# LITTLE LEAGUE SOFTBALL CHAMPS

**Joe Jackson**

# TABLE OF CONTENTS

*FOR MY BEAUTIFUL DAUGHTERS*

# ROLES TO PLAY

Emilee Davis reached for the new fastpitch softball bat and rubbed her hands along the smooth composite surface. The slender handle was coral in color, very easy to grip; the big barrel imprinted with black lettering. The 28-inch bat weighed 18 ounces and met the requirements of the new Little League Softball bat rules. Emilee held a firm grip on the new bat that fit into her small hands just right.

Stepping back to make sure there were no objects she might accidently hit, Emilee took a few easy swings. This balanced bat would hit a softball hard. It was very easy for her to swing and that was important. She knew she could swing this bat quickly and opposing fastpitch softball pitchers did not like quick bats. Without taking her gleaming eyes off it, she winked at her mom and turned to the sales clerk saying softly, 'It's a beauty and I'll take it."

The sales clerk grinned, walked behind the counter, and said, "I'll tell you what I'll do. If you promise to hit a home run, I will throw in a batting glove for you. What do you say about that?"

With a sparkle in her blue eyes, Emilee quickly replied, "With this bat I promise you and thank you so much for the glove."

Emilee had been saving as much money as she could for this purchase. She had earned money helping her neighbors and friends with odd jobs, baby sitting younger children, and handling the many responsibilities around her own home to earn an allowance. In the end though, she did have to count on a little help from her Mom and Dad.

She looked at her Mom and Dad, gave him a big hug, and said, "Isn't it a beauty, Dad? What do you think Mom? Thank you both so much for helping me."

Her Dad grinned from ear to ear and said, "If you hit one over the fence, I will give you an extra allowance and you and your mom can go do a little shopping."

"Okay," Emilee laughed as they left the store together. Ever since t-ball, she had not come close to hitting a home run, yet today she had made a promise to do just that. She looked at the bat again and smiled. She just knew in her heart that with this bat she would finally get one.

They hurried home quickly because tonight was a very important night. It was the opening night of Little League Softball and the first scheduled game was later this evening. After weeks of preparation, spring tryouts, and the many long, hard, sweaty practice sessions, Emilee was ready to play. Coach Wilson had asked for a brief meeting a few hours before game time.

The meeting was going to be at Emilee's house, on the patio. Earlier that morning, Emilee begged her mother not to furnish any soft drinks for the team. Her mother wanted to but Emilee was able to convince her that the team did not need to drink soft drinks before the start of the first game of the season.

"I just wanted to help keep the butterflies down and I thought a soda pop would help. But you are right Emilee," her mother said. "There is probably nothing in the world that will prevent butterflies on the opening night of Little League Softball."

Emilee sat down on one of the lawn chairs arranged on the patio. She was in full Purple Panther uniform, white with purple trim and purple leggings. Her purple cap, with the purple bill and button, was hanging from a peg on the wall. She was also wearing her new softball shoes, the ones with the latest molded cleat design. Her mother had surprised her with them the day before. *How her mother knew about the latest cleat style* Emilee had to wonder.

Little League Softball was softball for the youth, organized and established in 1974 with headquarters in Williamsport, Pennsylvania. Little League Softball was growing throughout the world, getting bigger and bigger every year with a final tournament schedule called the Little League Softball World Series. Each individual league had schedules with playoffs. The longer a team continued to win, the closer the team came to playing in the Little League Softball World Series Championship.

When her town announced it was organizing a Little League Softball league, Emilee was one of the first to appear at the ballpark to register. She enjoyed playing softball and could not wait to sign up. Various businesses and organizations in town sponsored the different teams by providing the uniforms and equipment to outfit each team. On the very first day of try-outs, with almost three hundred youngsters on the field, all of the different team coaches watching them carefully for selection decisions later, Emilee had been frantic with fear of going unnoticed after working so hard to show her own softball skills.

Later, at a special meeting the individual team coaches met to bid for the players they had reviewed and wanted. Each coach held a certain number of points to "purchase" the players they liked. This format had proven to be the best at preventing "cliquish" selections.

Coach Wilson of the Purple Panthers in the American League picked Emilee. In the beginning, she was not impressed with Coach Wilson even though coach did seem to know her softball. Emilee thought she looked rather dull. Her appearance was drab, her car a rust bucket, but after a few practice sessions, Emilee realized how focused Coach Wilson seemed to be as a Little League Softball coach. Emilee guessed being flashy was not a necessary coaching requirement.

Emilee's father saw her fidgeting in the chair and asked, "Are you nervous, Emilee?"

"A little," Emilee admitted.

"Don't worry one more bit about it, my little girl. You will get over it after you see the first pitch. Even big leaguers feel that way on opening night," her dad said. "Come with me to the front porch so you can greet your teammates as they arrive. Is the whole team coming this afternoon?"

Emilee nodded. "Coach Wilson called the meeting for four-thirty because that is when she gets off work. She couldn't make it any earlier."

"I see," her father murmured. "What about this Jennifer Wilson woman, your coach, Emilee? Where does she come from?"

"Other side of town," Emilee mumbled. There was not too much enthusiasm in her voice when she spoke of the Purple Panther coach and her father sensed it. Emilee had hoped the Pink Sox, managed by the former professional fastpitch outfielder, Melissa Williams, would select her. Of course, every one of the players on the field at tryouts that afternoon wanted to play for Coach Williams too.

"Was Wilson a softball player too?" her father asked as they went out on the porch.

"I think she played college softball and had a brief stint in a semi-pro league back in the 90's," Emilee said. "She's never talked about it."

"I suppose," her father murmured, "you wanted to play for Coach Williams, didn't you?"

Emilee moistened her lips. In a town like Lake Forbing with a population of just under thirty six thousand people, everybody knew Melissa Williams, because Melissa was the only professional softball player to come from the town. She had been good too, once up among the leading hitters and always a slick outfielder.

"I guess," Emilee admitted, "it would have been great playing for the Pink Sox. I would probably learn a lot more with Coach Williams."

Her father nodded. "You think so. Well, you know, sometimes the best ballplayers do not make the best coaches," he said. "Remember, whoever it is ever you play for, Emilee; always give them your best effort when you are practicing and playing on that ball field."

Two girls dressed in purple and white Purple Panther uniforms were coming down the street and

Emilee walked to the porch door to greet them. Her father touched her on the shoulder and walked into the living room. Emilee could hear him talking with her mother.

The girls coming up the walk were Hannah Miller, the right fielder, and Isabella Lopez, the catcher. Hannah was short with a solid build and had the wide shoulders of a swimmer. She was the hardest hitting batter on the team and had earned the fourth spot, called the cleanup, in the batting line-up. Hannah had very light blond hair and green eyes. She chewed gum vigorously and when she saw Emilee in the porch doorway, she lifted her hand and waved with a big smile.

Isabella Lopez, the catcher, also had a solid frame, though she was a little taller. Isabella was a tanned, olive-skinned girl with quick, capable hands, and a great throwing arm for a young girl of twelve. Coach Wilson always shook her head in amazement when she watched Isabella throw down to second.

Once on the porch Hannah asked, "Are we the first ones here, Emilee?"

"Well, yes you are," Emilee replied as she watched Isabella pick up the bat Emilee had just purchased from the store. Isabella held it in her hands while looking it over.

Hannah Miller moved over, sat down on the porch swing, and said, "I heard the Pink Sox had a meeting up at Melissa Williams' house yesterday. They say Melissa built a regular clubhouse in the back yard and filled it with all of her softball trophies, pictures, and souvenirs. Melissa calls it her "Softball House."

Emilee noticed an envious tone in Hannah's voice and said quickly, "The Pink Sox aren't going to win the pennant in Coach Williams' club house, Hannah. You know that."

"I know," Hannah admitted as she touched her chin thoughtfully.

Emilee glanced at Isabella who was still holding the new bat. Isabella, who lived across town in the tenement housing project, was from a large family of seven children besides herself and her father worked long hard hours in the railroad yards. Holding something new was not a common occurrence for Isabella, the youngest of her siblings. Isabella often claimed, jokingly, she was queen of the hand-me-downs.

Isabella sat down next to Hannah. She had a pretty face though she seldom smiled; a quiet, serious dark-eyed girl with long flowing black hair; a girl who had to really struggle with peer pressure to get out of her neighborhood and onto a Little League Softball team. Emilee had heard that most of the older kids from the tenement housing section teased Isabella for wanting to play on a Little League Softball team. Isabella had stood her ground and would have to stand some more ground because she often wore her softball uniform through the tenement housing project's streets as a proud representative of the Lake Forbing Purple Panthers. Isabella could handle it, though, Emilee thought. Besides that, coming from a large family,

Isabella had plenty of brothers, sisters, and cousins to support her.

Isabella said, "Everybody's late, Emilee."

"They'll be along," Emilee told her. She heard Isabella start to whistle softly, then Isabella said slowly,

"What do you think of Madelyn Taylor, Emilee?"

Emilee looked at her. "I guess Madelyn is all right," she said.

Madelyn Taylor was one of the four Purple Panther pitchers and easily the best from what Emilee had seen of her in practice sessions. Madelyn was from River Oaks out in the suburbs of Lake Forbing, and Emilee had learned that her father practically owned the big Lake Forbing Cotton Mills. The Taylor family had a summer home in the mountains and a winter home in Florida. They also had a big yacht because Madelyn had casually mentioned it one day during batting practice. She had invited Emilee down to the marina to help her clean the deck and Emilee had asked Madelyn, "How will I know which one is yours?" Madelyn had simply responded while walking away, "It is the only yacht in the harbor with a helicopter pad on it."

Emilee had sensed that Coach Wilson was curious to see how Isabella and Madelyn would get along. There had been no trouble between the two so far, but Emilee wondered how they were going to hit it off during the short Little League softball season of eighteen games, played during the summer vacation, with all of the games in the twilight of the evening.

An electrician's truck pulled up in front of the house, and two more girls in Purple Panther uniforms hopped out. Mr. Jones, a licensed electrician, grinned from behind the wheel, waved a hand to his daughter, Ashley, the Purple Panther left fielder, and then drove off to his next job.

With Ashley was little Sofia Hernandez, the youngest girl on the Purple Panther team. Sofia had just turned ten, was an amazingly fast runner, and under Coach Wilson's guidance, was developing into a dependable center fielder.

Sofia's father owned a little Mexican restaurant on the main street in downtown Lake Forbing. The food was excellent there, especially the homemade tamales and her mother's famous flan dessert. Mr. Hernandez wanted to sponsor one of the teams even though his restaurant, a very small, one-window affair, was not making a great deal of money. Because other sponsors had put their bids in first, his offer, though appreciated, was not accepted.

Ashley Jones, tall, slender, and ash-blond nodded to Emilee when she came up. She pointed and said, "Look, there's Madison Moore."

Madison, the third baseman, was coming up the street from one direction, and Sarah Anderson, the shortstop, from the opposite direction. Moore was taller of the two girls, green-eyed, with a cute splash of freckles on her face surrounded by her curly, red hair.

So far, Emilee felt some tension existed between Moore and Sarah Anderson. Sarah was a quiet shy girl, and Madison Moore, just the opposite, took it for a lack of self-esteem.

Jasmine Brown, the first baseman for the team, followed behind Moore. Jasmine appeared a little self-conscious in her uniform while walking the streets of Emilee's neighborhood where she very seldom came. Like Lopez, Johnson lived in the same tenement housing project and had to put in just as much effort as Lopez to get onto the Little League Softball team. She was another quiet girl, but very good at fielding balls and digging throws out of the dirt at first. Jasmine had a beautiful infectious smile and Emilee had liked her immediately upon meeting her.

Madison Moore jumped up on the porch and said rather sourly, "Coach Wilson here, yet?"

"She'll be along," Emilee assured her. "She told me she might be a few minutes late."

Madison sat down on the edge of the porch. She took the bat from Isabella Lopez's hands and examined it, her green eyes shining a little. "This is a beauty," she murmured.

"Here's Coach Wilson now," Hannah Miller said.

The players on the porch lapsed into silence as Coach Wilson stepped off the bus on the corner and hurried toward the house, checking the house numbers as she walked, not sure which one was Emilee's. She was tall, in her thirties, but very skinny, almost bony, a homely looking woman.

When she saw the girls on the porch, she waved while smiling and Emilee went out to meet her.

"How are you, Emilee?" the Purple Panther coach said.

She had a nice smile, very warm, which made Emilee forget her rather homely face. "Is everybody here?" Coach Wilson asked.

Three more Purple Panther pitchers – Destiny Johnson, Samantha Smith, and Maria Rodriguez, were hurrying around the corner. These three girls, with Madelyn Taylor, filled out the pitching roster.

"Everybody's here but Madelyn," Madison Moore told her.

"Well, we'll give Madelyn five more minutes," Coach Wilson said cheerily. "Is this group all set for the big opener this evening?"

The players all nodded, but Emilee could see that there was not too much enthusiasm. Most of the players, she herself included, wanted to be playing for the famous Melissa Williams. Emilee was a little ashamed, remembering her thoughts. It was not fair to Coach Wilson, who was working very hard with this team, getting it ready for the opening game, while also working full time at her job to make her own living.

Emilee stood back against one of the porch columns, looking at the various players. With the exception of Destiny Johnson, the pitcher, and Ashley Jones, the outfielder, she had known none of the others before the team formed. They were all from different parts of Lake Forbing because the league had held open tryouts. The eight coaches, representing the eight teams in the Lake Forbing Leagues, had made their choices from the various players at spring tryouts without any knowledge of a player's background, judging them solely upon their abilities on the diamond.

Coach Wilson's selections, without her knowing it at the time, had cut right through Lake Forbing society. From the walled, gated communities like River Oaks where Madelyn Taylor lived, to the middle class residential neighborhoods like Emilee's, to the tenement housing project on the other side of the railroad tracks. Emilee's neighborhood included shopkeepers in town like the Anderson's, the electrician Jones, and the Hernandez family, who owned the restaurant. It included working-class men like Mr. Moore and Mr. Miller.

Coach had mentioned at their first practice session, "Each one of you is different with a different role to play. If we learn how to work and play together, we can be counted on like a fine tuned engine."

A luxurious black touring car was pulling up to the curb with a chauffeur at the wheel. When the car came to a stop, the chauffeur stepped out and opened the door. Madelyn Taylor bounced out, grinning like everyone else, already in her full Purple Panther uniform.

"Holy smoke," little Sofia Hernandez gasped. "This girl has her own chauffer!"

Madelyn came up on the porch, a very pretty girl, with honey blond hair and beautiful blue eyes. Everyone often said Madelyn and Emilee looked so much alike they could pass for sisters.

"How is it everybody?" Madelyn grinned. "Sorry I am late. We just got back from the beach and George had to rush me over here."

Emilee noticed that George, the chauffeur, had taken out his eBook reader and was preparing to read as he sat behind the wheel. Evidently, he intended to wait for Madelyn.

The other girls were looking at the car, also. Jasmine Brown touched her chin thoughtfully, her eyes wide. Isabella Lopez's face was expressionless and Emilee did not know what to think.

"Since we are all here," Coach Wilson said, "let's start the meeting."

They went out to the patio and sat down in the chairs. Coach started to talk as soon as they sat down. She spoke briskly, often using her hands to emphasize a point.

"We have a good team here," she said earnestly, "a very good team. I do not know how far we will go in this league, but if we all pull together, we can do some wonderful things. I have seen some very good teams fall apart because they could not or would not play together. It is not how good you are in softball or any team sport, but it's how well you play alongside the person next to you."

Tall, slender Ashley Jones was nodding her head vigorously. Little Sofia Hernandez nodded also, taking her cue from Jones, who was her best friend forever.

The other girls just looked at Coach Wilson or at the floor. Emilee could see the talk was not making too much of an impression on anyone.

"Okay then," coach finished. "Here's the lineup for tonight's twilight game." Earlier in the week, during practice, Coach Wilson had announced that Madelyn would start the first softball game.

She posted a scrap of paper on the wall showing all positions filled with Madelyn Taylor pitching and Isabella Lopez catching. Silent murmurs grew louder and excitement began to build. You could feel it in the air. The first game of the season was about to start.

"One other thing," coach said. "We'll need a team captain and that is somebody you will have to elect yourselves.

Sofia Hernandez said, "How about Emilee Davis?"

Hannah Miller, Ashley Jones, and Sarah Anderson nodded.

"Anybody else nominated?" Coach asked.

There were no other nominations and Emilee became the team captain. Coach Wilson whispered to her quietly, "Okay, Emilee, it's your job, and good luck with it. You would have been my choice too."

"Thanks," Emilee murmured. She shifted uneasily on her feet, wondering how much luck she was going to need. She was now the team captain of the Lake Forbing Purple Panthers, a team with a coach most of the players had no respect for at all and the first game of the season was just moments away.

## TIME TO PLAY

There was a parade out to the park for the opening games of the Little League season. A fire department ladder truck and a police car, both with their lights flashing, and one of the area high school bands marched ahead, leading the procession. Local league officials, sponsors, organizations, and town dignitaries followed the band with the individual teams, their players in full uniforms, marching behind, carrying their team banners covered with the names of their sponsors.

A smiling Emilee carried one end of the Purple Panther banner and a proud Isabella carried the other. It looked as if the whole town had turned out to watch the parade march to the new ball field, a field specially constructed for the Little League Softball games. Groups of kids had even come down from across the railroad tracks. Many were jeering as the teams went by. Several of them pointed and hooted at Isabella and Jasmine in their new uniforms as they walked past. Both girls held their heads high and their jaws tight while staring straight ahead.

Coach Wilson walked with the Purple Panthers, grinning while looking a little self-conscious, trying to keep step with the rest of the parade marchers.

Up ahead of the Purple Panthers walked the Pink Sox, with Melissa Williams marching ahead of them alone, smiling, and waving her hand to the crowd. She wore a nice athletic sports outfit with new sport shoes and her long black hair parted in the middle. She seemed cool, clean, efficient, and very confident.

Looking over at Coach Wilson, Emilee noticed a striking difference. Coach wore a rather baggy pair of pants made of a dark polyester material. Her white shirt frayed at the collar, her blouse sleeves rolled up, and her ordinary black loafers looked rather worse for wear.

Emilee remembered what she had heard so many times from coach about the appearance of an opposing team. "Get it out of your head girls," coach had said, "because just like you, they put their uniforms on one leg at a time. Without a person inside it, a uniform would just lie on the floor and gather dust."

At the ball field, the band played the Star Spangled Banner, the Little League representative made a short speech, and then the Purple Panthers took the field with the Pink Sox at bat. The big crowd that had swarmed after the parade filled the bleachers behind the dugouts and the home plate fence. The smell of popcorn and hotdogs from the concession stand was definitely in the air. The ball field was buzzing with something. Emilee knew what it was: LITTLE LEAGUE SOFTBALL EXCITEMENT!

After a brief warm-up session of stretching and throwing, the plate umpire tossed a white official Little League softball out on the field.

Madelyn Taylor, smiling broadly and looking very cool and calm, walked out to the pitcher's circle and picked up the ball. In Little League Softball games, especially fastpitch, a good pitcher controlled, and runs were generally hard to come by. Madelyn had proved to be that kind of pitcher in practice sessions. She would prove it today, Emilee hoped.

Isabella Lopez stood behind the plate, her mask on the ground beside her, staring out at Taylor, waiting for her warm-up pitches. Emilee trotted out to second base. Madison Moore moved quickly to third base, Sarah Anderson trotted to shortstop, and tall Jasmine Brown eased over to first.

The three Purple Panther outfielders, Hannah Miller, Sofia Hernandez, and Ashley Jones, sprinted toward their outfield positions. Destiny Johnson, because she was not pitching, eased out to her "rover" position. The umpire bawled from behind home plate, "PLAY BALL."

Emilee felt the nervous energy rising inside of her and she could hardly stand still. Her father and mother sat in the stands on the first base side of the field, along with one of her uncles, her aunt, and her grandmother. Every other player on the field had relatives present except Isabella Lopez. Isabella had informed Emilee that there would be no one there to watch her play. Her father was busy playing soccer and did not want to be bothered with softball. Her mom had to stay with her brother.

Madelyn Taylor's parents, with a few of their friends present, sat apart from the others at the far end of the third base stands. They dressed in fine expensive looking sports clothes, and Madelyn's father, a big, heavy-set man with a bulldog face, who did not look at all like his pretty daughter, smoked a big fat cigar.

Coach Wilson stayed in the Purple Panther dugout with the substitutes. Emilee could see that even she was nervous. First, she sat on the dugout steps, rubbing her hands; then she stood, and then she sat down again.

The first Pink Sox batter put on the protective helmet and walked out to the plate. Madelyn stood on the pitching rubber, watching her, waiting for Isabella's signal. Isabella had her mask, chest protector, and kneepads on now. She squatted down, stared at Madelyn through the bars of her mask, and then flashed her signal for the fastball.

Madelyn wound up and her strong athletic body lunged forward as she pitched, her foot in constant contact with the pitching rubber until she released the softball. The Pink Sox batter swung at the new white ball. It bounced one time toward third base. Madison Moore caught it before it could bounce again and threw it across to first. Her throw was a little wild, but Jasmine Brown stretched her long frame out, keeping her toe on the bag and the base umpire waved the runner out.

Emilee felt a little better as the big crowd yelled encouragement while applauding the play. The second Pink Sox batter walked to the plate. The public address system, with the announcer calling out the name of each player, made the second batter appear a little uncomfortable. She grinned sheepishly while walking up to the plate.

Madelyn, pitching effortlessly, got two strikes over on her and then the Pink Sox batter hit a ground ball down to Sarah Anderson at short. Sarah rushed the ball and it went through her legs.

Emilee raced over to second to cover on the throw in from the outfield and saw little Sofia Hernandez let the ball go through her legs also and the crown howled as the Pink Sox runner sprinted around the bases for a run, the ball rolling out to the center-field fence.

Emilee felt sick. She looked over at Sarah who was kicking at the ground, her face pale. Madison Moore was scowling on third, pounding her glove and Emilee had a good idea what Madison thought of Sarah.

Out in center field little Sofia looked as if she were ready to cry. On what should have been an infield out a Pink Sox player had scored a run, putting the Pink Sox ahead, one to nothing.

Madelyn was not pleased either. She scowled from the pitcher's circle as she prepared to pitch again. She bore down hard, striking out the two Pink Sox batters, each on three straight pitches, to retire the side.

Emilee heard Madison Moore say bitterly as they came into the dugout, "What do you expect? We'll never get anywhere with her at short."

Sarah heard the remark and her face was red and as she went out to bat, leading off for the Purple Panthers.

Coach Wilson said quietly, "Okay, gang. Let us not worry about one run. We will get it back. Everybody in there now, talk it up."

Sarah struck out, swinging at a very high pitch. She came back to the dugout dragging her bat. Emilee, who was second in the batting order, stepped up to the plate with her throat very dry.

Destiny Johnson, who was down in the third base coaching box yelled, "Start us off, Emilee."

The Pink Sox pitcher was a left-hander and she threw hard. Coach Wilson called from the dugout,

"Make her put it over, Emilee."

Emilee gripped her new bat tightly, watching the pitcher. The first pitch was right over the heart of the plate and she swung hard. There was a resounding and distinctive metal "tink" as the composite bat met the ball cleanly and the ball arched out over second base, the first clean hit of the evening as well as the first clean hit of the new Little League Softball season!

The crowd yelled and the Purple Panther players in the dugout screamed. Maria Rodriguez, coaching from first, pounded Emilee's back happily.

Jasmine Brown walked to the plate and looked at the dugout for her signal from Coach Wilson. They had worked out a very nice set of signals for the season. Each player had her own spot depending on her place in the lineup that coach would touch for that players' signal. One touch on your spot while you were batting meant bunt, while one touch on your spot when you were on base meant steal.

Coach's right knee was for spot number one, her right hip number two, the inside of her right elbow the third spot, and her right shoulder number four. The top of Coach's head was the fifth spot and the remaining spots went down her left side just like the right side for spots six, seven, eight, and nine. Since Jasmine was the third batter in the lineup, her spot would be inside the right elbow of Coach Wilson. If coach did not touch that spot, it meant Jasmine could hit away.

A player really had to pay attention because coach would touch five to seven different spots before every pitch. Emilee thought it was probably a good way for coach to handle her game time energy and an excellent way to keep each player focused.

Jasmine Brown looked down at Emilee as Emilee stood on the base. Then she tugged at her cap and took the first pitch for a ball. Jasmine swung at the second pitch and hit a long fly to center field. The Pink Sox center fielder caught it for the second out with Hannah coming up for the Purple Panthers.

In the Purple Panther dugout, coach had touched her left hip while flashing signs to Emilee and Emilee knew exactly what that meant. Emilee touched her cap to signal that she had caught the steal sign from coach. The Pink Sox left-hander was watching her carefully and the big Pink Sox catcher pounded her glove, both of them sure she was going to steal.

Starting with the first movement of the left-handed pitcher towards home, the way coach had taught them in practice, Emilee had a good jump on her, and she needed it. She ran as hard as she could and slid on her hip as she neared the bag. The catcher's throw was there but the second baseman dropped the ball as Emilee slid into the bag.

"Safe," yelled the field ump.

The Purple Panthers on the bench yelled happily and then they screamed when Hannah swung at the next pitch, hitting it over the left field fence for a home run. The fence was one hundred and seventy five feet away and the ball had no problem clearing it by another twenty feet.

The Purple Panther fans in the stands stood up, cheering as Hannah proudly loped around the bases, pumping her fist as she came into home because her home run put the Purple Panthers into the lead 2 to 1.

Emilee slapped Hannah's back as she came into the dugout and she heard Hannah say softly,

"That's one."

Emilee glanced at her, not particularly liking the statement. It was not one, but two runs for the Purple Panthers, but it sounded as if Hannah was not thinking about the Purple Panther runs; she was thinking about herself and the big gold trophy awarded to the girl hitting the most home runs in the Lake Forbing Little League Softball league at the end of the season. To Hannah it was, therefore, one home run.

In the third inning, the Pink Sox tied up the score on an error by Sarah at short. With a runner on third and two out, Sarah bobbled the ball in the infield, letting the runner come in.

Madison Moore had a fit on third base. She kicked at the dirt again and she shook her head in disgust. She looked over at Coach Wilson as if the fault were hers for putting Sarah in the game.

"Shake it off, forget it," coach called from the dugout. "We'll get it back."

Madelyn was also fuming in the pitching circle because two unearned runs had scored and Madelyn was pitching a good game, having given up only one clean hit so far.

Emilee trotted in to the circle to have a word with Madelyn and said, "Don't let it worry you, Madelyn."

"I can't strike them all out," Madelyn complained. "I need support out there too."

Emilee saw Isabella Lopez watching the pitcher grimly, hands on her hips. "Play ball,' Isabella called tersely from the plate.

The game got under way again and Madelyn retired the side with no more runs. Trouble broke out in the Purple Panther dugout, however, when the Purple Panthers came in at the end of the inning. Madison Moore made another remark and this time Sarah came back at her. Sarah said quietly,

"I don't have to take that from you, Madison."

The redhead looked at her. "Is that what you think?" she murmured.

"Yes," Sarah snapped. "I'm not afraid of you."

"Maybe we..." Madison started to say and then Coach Wilson came in between them saying with a good-natured smile, "Let's forget it." Coach then looked around the dugout and said, "We're all pals here."

Emilee saw the troubled look deep down in the tall woman's eyes, however, and she realized coach was worried. This different mix of girls, this collection of different characters, seemed to be cracking up in the first game of the season.

In the fifth inning, the Pink Sox scored two more runs and there was an error this time by Jasmine Brown at first base. Madelyn Taylor walked out of the circle in disgust at the end of the inning with the score 4 to 2 for the Pink Sox.

It was still 4 to 2 in the bottom of the sixth and last inning, with the game apparently in the bag for the Pink Sox. The Pink Sox left-hander, ably coached by Melissa Williams, had pitched a beautiful softball game so far, allowing only three hits while walking two players. Isabella Lopez had doubled in the fourth inning, but she stayed there, stranded on second base.

Across the field, Melissa Williams sat in her dugout, smiling, very pleased with her first Pink Sox victory, or so she must have thought. Then the Purple Panthers pounced. Madison Moore, leading off, singled over first base, her first hit in the league, and she ran down to the bag, yelling at the top of her lungs.

Coach Wilson immediately called for a bunt because little Sofia Hernandez bunted very well and could run like a deer. Sofia dropped the bunt along third base and shot away from home plate with the speed of an arrow. She was past the bag when the first baseman caught the throw and both girls were safe.

The Purple Panther fans started to make noise in the stands. Isabella Lopez was coming up and Isabella had hit the ball hard the last time up. She was going to hit it again; you could feel it. Emilee could tell from the way she stood there, with her legs braced and her bat still on her shoulder, just staring at the pitcher. She was hitting away and that she did, on the first pitch, driving the ball through the left center field gap, scoring Moore and putting Hernandez on third. She went into second for her second double of the evening. The score was now 4 to 3 for the Pink Sox.

Melissa Williams came out of the dugout, no longer smiling, muttering under her breath. She called for time and she had a few words with her left-hander. Madelyn, a very good batter, was up to hit, but this time she would not hit the ball very far. Her roller back to the pitcher was the first out of the inning. Sofia held at third after being looked back by the Pink Sox pitcher.

With one out, the Pink Sox intentionally walked Sarah Anderson, loading the bases to set up for a double play that would retire the side and win the game.

Emilee, next girl in line to bat, crouched in the batter on-deck circle, watching while they intentionally walked Sarah. Coach Wilson came out to talk to her as Sarah trotted down to first base.

The crowd was yelling now. Emilee could see her father standing up, watching her. She held in her hands the new bat her father had helped her purchase that afternoon, the same with which she had hit her single earlier in the game. She had to hit again now or the Purple Panthers would go down to their first defeat.

Coach Wilson said quietly, "You can hit this girl, Emilee. You have hit her before. Make her put it over the plate in your zone. Do not try to crush it. All we need is a base hit to win the game. Just put your bat on the ball. The ball will go all by itself."

"All right," Emilee muttered. She was nervous now, her legs weak, and her hands sweating. She rubbed dirt on the bat and she stepped into the batter's box.

Melissa Williams was calling to the pitcher, "C'mon, c'mon. You've got this girl, Josie."

Emilee really resented that remark and she stepped back out of the box to clear her mind of it. She had to focus. Even though Coach Williams already considered her out, Emilee wanted very much to beat the ex-pro and her Pink Sox who most people in town thought would win this softball game and dominate the Lake Forbing American league.

The left-handed Pink Sox pitcher was on the pitching rubber, looking at her and then she started her wind up. The softball came in a little wide of the plate. Emilee let it go for a called ball.

She adjusted her batting helmet and dug in again, remembering Coach Wilson's words. She was to just meet the ball, get the barrel of her bat on it solidly and the softball would do the rest.

The next pitch was a riser and Emilee swung at it, fouling it back into the backstop behind the catcher, making the count one and one. The entire Purple Panther team was on the dugout steps, yelling for that hit now and the Pink Sox were chattering in the infield.

Emilee dug in at the plate. She was not as tall as Jasmine Brown, nor as solidly built as Hannah Miller or Madison Moore; but, she was not weak and she could hit a ball pretty far when she caught hold of it. She stepped out of the box and thought about the left field fence one hundred seventy five feet away. A home run with the bases loaded, a grand slam in her first game of Little League Softball would really be something, but then she remembered Coach Wilson's comment. The Purple Panthers did not need a home run to win this game. A base hit would be perfect.

The left-hander threw another pitch and it was again outside for a ball. Emilee stepped outside the box and looked over at Coach Wilson. The Purple Panther coach just smiled at her confidently, pointing toward the outfield.

The next pitch was in her zone and Emilee swung. She literally saw the ball hit the bat barrel; she heard the distinctive "tink" sound in her ears and her heart leaped with joy as the softball darted between shortstop and third base, rolling to the outfield.

As she raced madly toward first base, she heard the roar of the crowd from the stands. Two Purple Panther runners pounded over the plate and then all of the Purple Panther players raced out to first base to pound and jump on Emilee's back. Emilee saw her father standing up, shouting, and grinning.

"You did it, Emilee!" Madison Moore howled. "That's number one for the Purple Panthers."

Walking back to the dugout and seeing the smiling Coach Wilson, Emilee Davis was thinking Little League Softball was so much. Her team, the Lake Forbing Purple Panthers, was the best of the eight teams in their league, maybe best in their district, maybe best in their section, or maybe the best fastpitch softball team in the whole world!

# CHAOS

They won another game that week, beating the Eagles in a 10 to 2 score with Destiny Johnson pitching for the Purple Panthers. Hannah Miller hit her second home run over the center field fence. Isabella Lopez also hit a home run and Madison Moore came through with four hits in five times at bat.

At the end of the week, the league standings appeared in the Lake Forbing newspaper and Emilee studied them carefully, as she sat at home in the finished basement with Destiny Johnson, Madison Moore, and little Sofia Hernandez. The American League standings showed the Purple Panthers undefeated and leading their league. Melissa Williams' Pink Sox were in last place.

Destiny Johnson pointed with her finger at the paper and she said to Emilee slyly, "What do you think of Melissa Williams' Pink Sox now, Emilee?"

Emilee just shook her head perplexed. The Pink Sox lost their first two games and were now in last place in the American League standings.

"Everybody wanted to play for Coach Williams," Madison grinned, "but you'll notice Coach Wilson's team is on top."

"We'll stay there too," Sofia said slowly. "We're going to win the pennant in this league and then we're going to beat the winners of the National League in Lake Forbing and then….."

"Hey," Madison broke in laughing. "We've only played two games so far, Sofia. We might lose the next ten."

Little Sofia shook her head. "We have the two best pitchers in the league," she stated, "in Madelyn Taylor and Destiny here, and we have the best hitters."

Emilee sat on one of the basement benches listening to the talk. It was Saturday morning and with no league games scheduled for the day, Coach Wilson had called a practice session at the park grounds for that afternoon.

"Lots of things we have to work out here," coach told them after the Eagles win. "Some of you girls aren't hitting well enough yet and the infield is a little sloppy, especially the throwing. Then there is bunting, base stealing, and sliding techniques that we really need to work on. It always helps us to practice whenever we can. We have to get the fundamentals down. We have to be fundamentally sound out there on the field."

It was a hot and humid Saturday in early July as the Purple Panther squad straggled down to the park playing field. When Emilee arrived with Destiny Johnson from her block, she found Madison, Isabella, and Hannah sitting on the bench waiting for them.

Sarah was playing catch with Jasmine Brown out on the field. Maria Rodriguez and Samantha Smith were just coming up from the water cooler, sweaty and dusty. Coach Wilson drove up in a shabby little roadster she had just bought. It was painted green, at least fifteen years old and it made a great deal of noise as she rolled into the parking lot nearby. It was a real rust-bucket.

Emilee saw Hannah Miller and Madison Moore eyeing the old car thoughtfully and then Hannah said, "Old junk-heap. Did you see Melissa Williams' big SUV? She can get the whole team in it, almost."

"Well, that SUV can't hit, can't field, and certainly can not throw a softball so that big SUV will never win a ballgame," Madison said from the other end of the bench. Madison had just arrived and was putting on her new softball shoes, a nice pair with the molded cleat design that all the players seemed to be raving about these days. Madison's father had bought her the shoes after the outfielder had made three hits in the Eagle game.

Coach Wilson hustled up. She wore baggy slacks, a faded blue shirt with the sleeves rolled up and a softball cap. As usual, she was smiling broadly, clapping her hands, full of pep. She said,

"What do you think about a little batting practice right now, gang? I want you to think about your hitting zone, concentrating and expecting a pitch in your zone every time you get up to bat. Maria, you can do the pitching for us." Then she looked at Emilee and said, "Everybody here Captain?"

"Everybody, except Madelyn," Emilee told her while looking around.

Coach nodded. "Madelyn can not make it this afternoon," she said, wiping the perspiration from her face. "She texted me earlier in the day to confirm that she had other plans."

Isabella, who had been putting on her kneepads to catch for batting practice stopped, looked at the Purple Panther coach steadily and asked, "Why?"

Coach shrugged, "Her family left for the weekend and Madelyn had to go along with them."

Emilee saw Isabella's lips tighten and there was a grim smile on her face as she walked to the plate. Emilee heard her say,

"Must be nice to be down at the beach on such a hot day like this? Too bad we all can't go."

Emilee said quickly, "I think Madelyn would much rather be here with us, Isabella. She couldn't help it if her folks decided to leave town for the weekend."

"Okay," Isabella snickered. "I didn't mean anything, Emilee."

Emilee trotted out to second base and she watched as Coach Wilson worked with Sarah and Jasmine at the plate. Neither player had done much as of yet and Sarah had been especially weak, striking out four times in the two games played.

Coach worked patiently with her skinny shortstop, getting her to change her style of batting. Sarah had been taking a full wild swing at the pitches, but coach was trying to get her to shorten her bat by choking up on it. Coach wanted Sarah to punch at the ball as it came in, just meet it with the bat barrel. Coach kept repeating, "Let the bat barrel do the work for you."

It took a while for Sarah to catch on and the players in the field were getting impatient. Madison, waiting out in deep short, slapped her glove a few times and kept muttering to herself that coach had made a big mistake signing Sarah with the club and that they'd do better to trade her to the lowly Eagles, or even down to the lower league in Lake Forbing, a league comprised of younger, less capable ball players.

Emilee edged over toward the redhead and she said quietly, "If Sarah hears you talking like that, Madison, it'll be harder for her. Sarah is trying and she is a good infielder.

Moore laughed jeeringly. "Can't hit, can't field, and can't run. What's she good for?"

Madison had just said the words "good for" when Sarah lined a nice ball right between Madison and Emilee. Sarah managed to hit a few more balls sharply before coach sent her out to the field and went to work with the tall Jasmine Brown.

Sarah was not sure just where to go as she came out on the field with her glove. She looked at Madison, who was standing at short and then she started out to the outfield. As she went past the redhead, Emilee heard Moore say something. Emilee did not make out the words, but the remark could not have been complimentary.

Sarah stopped and her face turned red. She stared at Madison for one long moment and Emilee started to walk that way, thinking Sarah was going to make an issue out of it. Sarah then turned and walked away, looking down at the ground.

Jasmine was another gate swinger and Emilee heard Coach Wilson say to her patiently, "Keep your eyes on the ball, Jasmine. Don't ever take your eyes off the ball when it's coming toward the plate."

Jasmine's weakness was swinging the bat from the shoulder. Coach had her drop the bat a little as the ball started to come in. This adjustment caused Jasmine to swing level and she no longer had the chopping swing she had been taking. Her swing now looked very fluid.

Suddenly a loud metal noise was heard, not a "tink" but a "tunk" sound. They were all very surprised to see that Jasmine had finally caught hold of a ball and hit it far over Hannah's head in center field. Coach Wilson slapped Jasmine on the back as she left the plate. Jasmine was grinning with that big beautiful smile.

Madison said to Emilee, "That girl is going to be a hitter. Hannah Miller has never hit a softball that far in her whole life."

Emilee nodded, very happy that Jasmine seemed to be making strides. She played next to her on the infield and she had come to like her very much. Jasmine was quiet, but she gave her best all the time and she was working very hard on her fundamentals at first base.

They had infield practice after the batting session and Emilee was amazed at some of the stops Sarah made. Sarah covered a great deal of ground at short and her throws to first were hard and accurate. Madison Moore, on the other hand, was just the opposite on her throws to first from third. Wild and inaccurate, to describe her throws across the diamond, would be an understatement. "Where is Madison's head?" Emilee wondered to herself.

For thirty minutes, coach batted ground balls to each fielder while watching the way they handled the balls, making positive suggestions. Her blue shirt became sweat stained, yet her enthusiasm never let up and Emilee could definitely see the improvement on the field after a while.

Coach then trotted out to second base, letting Destiny Johnson hit the infield grounders. She worked with Emilee and Sarah on double plays at second, showing them exactly how they were to handle the throws as they touched the bag while turning to whip the ball across to first.

Sarah had the habit of trying to get rid of the ball almost before she caught Emilee's throw and as a result, she threw wildly or dropped the ball, ruining the play. Coach worked with her to slow down.

"Keep the runner off of second base. Make sure we get her out before we try for the next one," coach grinned. "Work too fast and we lose both runners. We have to get the lead runner out coming down from first. She is the most important. Keeping runners off second base is very important in this game of softball. Remember that."

She taught Emilee how to whip the ball across the letters of her shirt, dragging her foot over the bag while taking Sarah's throw and after a while, it became very smooth.

"Don't worry," said coach. "We'll get better. When you've done it a couple of thousand times you will be doing it in your sleep."

They had sliding practice after that and coach taught them how to hit the dirt, doing it herself a half dozen times, demonstrating how they had to move in toward the bag in the hook slide, falling away from the infielder's tag, leaving only the tip of the cleats, to hook the bag with one toe.

The Purple Panther coach was dirty and dusty when she got up to watch the players do it, her face streaked with sweat and dust. Nevertheless, she was smiling broadly, really enjoying her time here.

The players lined up and slid into the bag one after the other with Coach Wilson standing by, watching each one, correcting them, and showing them how to avoid a "strawberry." By keeping your hip slightly elevated until the slide finished, you protected yourself from developing a red abrasion, or a strawberry, at the hipbone. Sofia Hernandez proved to be the best slider on the team. The small girl could run like the wind and she quickly caught on to the hook slide, literally flying into the bag, then fading away.

Isabella Lopez proved to be another good slider. Isabella was the reckless type, tearing into the base high and hard, and hitting the break away bag with great force. When she got up after one of her slides, she looked at Emilee grimly and said,

"You know, it is a lot cooler down at the beach, Emilee?"

Emilee slapped her on the back. "Forget about it, Isabella," she smiled.

"Si, si!" Isabella grinned sheepishly.

Madison Moore did not like Sarah and Emilee noticed that Hannah would watch Jasmine Brown occasionally, nonchalantly, with a small frown on Hannah's wide face. Hannah was the acknowledged home run hitter of this team, gunning for the big trophy and now one of her own teammates had suddenly demonstrated that she could hit a very long ball too. Jasmine might well begin to challenge Hannah for the honor.

The practice session broke up at four-thirty. Coach Wilson climbed into her "new" old jalopy, dirty and sweaty, smiled and waved to the team, and then drove away. Emilee gathered at the water cooler with the other players for a good drink of cold water before walking home with Destiny Johnson.

It was at the water cooler that the tension between Anderson and Moore broke out into the open. Sarah was having a drink when the redhead came up, swaggering a little, with her glove dangling from her fingertips. Emilee sensed trouble immediately and she looked around quickly to see the taillights of Coach Wilson's car disappear around the corner. With the Purple Panther coach gone, it was up to her as team captain to keep things in hand.

Moore said evenly, "Okay Sarah, hurry it up."

Sarah had just started to drink and she was thirsty. She lifted her head slightly and put it back down to the water cooler. Moore lifted her glove and slapped it hard across Sarah's back. She said tersely,

"You heard what I said."

Sarah straightened up, her face white and Emilee eased over to them hastily.

"There's plenty of water here, Madison," she protested. "Let's not start any trouble."

Madison Moore said grimly, "Move away, Anderson."

Sarah said slowly, "No."

Moore pushed her hard then backed away, dropping her glove. Sarah straightened up and rushed at Madison, in a full-blown rage. She slapped the redhead a few times in the face, light blows, and then Moore, known as one tough cat, knocked her down with several sharp-fisted punches to Sarah's face.

Emilee moved in between them, grasping the strong redhead's arms. She said pleadingly, "Look, Madison, we can't have fights on this team. It is not good. Sarah's one of our players. You are both on the same team."

Sarah got to her feet, blood trickling from her cut mouth. She did not back down. She came around Emilee, tears of rage in her eyes, knowing that she was going to take a licking from the bigger, stronger girl, but she was not afraid.

Moore broke away from Emilee and as Sarah rushed at her, they met with a flurry of energy, Sarah getting the worst of it again, trying to hold her ground, fighting back hard as she could, but having to retreat as Moore kept charging her.

Again, Emilee broke in between them and this time Isabella helped her. Emilee had not anticipated

Isabella as a source of help, figuring others did not want to have the spiteful Moore turn on them.

Isabella said sourly, "Cut it out, Madison. You can lick this girl with one hand. Let it go at that."

Moore stepped back, pushing Emilee's hands away. She said to Isabella, her face flushed, angry, green eyes wild, "Keep out of this, you twit."

Isabella looked at her. "Don't call me that," she said slowly.

"Listen," Emilee begged. "We can't have this whole team fighting."

"She's tough," Madison sneered. "Let's see how tough she is." She had forgotten about Sarah, recognizing the fact that Isabella, her own size and with a reputation of her own as a tough one, was a better match.

Ashley Jones called suddenly, "Here comes a park attendant. We all better get out of here now."

The park attendant had seen the fight between Sarah and Madison and was walking briskly toward them from across the field. His presence broke up both fights. Madison left with Hannah. Isabella, her catcher's equipment under her arm, started north across the railroad tracks. Jasmine Brown went with her while the others split up in different directions, going to their homes. No doubt, now, there was bad blood between Moore and Lopez, the two toughest girls on the Purple Panther team and two of the best players.

Later that night at dinner Emilee's mother said to her, "Well, with two straight wins in the league it looks like your Purple Panthers are going to make a clean sweep of the American League and get into the playoffs."

Emilee looked at her glumly.

"No?" her mother asked curiously. "Are you having any trouble, Emilee?"

*Trouble,* Emilee thought miserably, *is not the word for it. CHAOS sounded much better.*

"Tell me about it," her mom urged.

Emilee told her the story of the fight at the park and the remarks Isabella Lopez made about Madelyn Taylor.

"I don't think it's just because Madelyn's father is rich and Isabella's father is poor," Emilee muttered. "It goes deeper than that."

"Some girls just do not hit it off with other girls," her mother said, nodding sympathetically. "I can see you have a problem on your hands, Emilee, but keep your chin up. Things always look worse than they really are. When this team of yours really starts clicking you'll see a big difference."

Emilee hoped fervently that this was so.

## GET RID OF HER

On Monday evening, they played the Diamond Divas, the team that had beaten Melissa Williams' team a few days before. Coach Wilson had Madelyn Taylor back in the pitcher's circle. For three innings, Madelyn was superb, not allowing a hit and striking out four batters.

The Purple Panthers broke the game wide open in the third inning when Sarah, hitting the way coach had taught her, punched a single to right field. Emilee dropped down a nice sacrifice bunt to advance Sarah to second and then Jasmine hit a ball over the left-field fence for her first fastpitch softball home run.

Most of the Purple Panther players whooped it up in the dugout, but Emilee noticed Hannah standing out at home plate, watching Jasmine round the bases, hearing the crowd applaud. Hannah was not smiling. When Jasmine crossed the plate, Hannah was swinging two bats, looking the other way. She said nothing.

Hannah swung at a bad pitch and lifted a weak foul to third base that the Diamond Diva third baseman caught easily. Hannah came back to the dugout, scowling, shaking her head in disgust.

Coach Wilson said to her cheerfully, "Don't let them get you on those bad pitches, Hannah. Make 'em put the ball in your zone, then hit it hard."

"Okay," Hannah said stiffly. "Okay."

It was 2 to 0 for the Purple Panthers going into the fourth with Madelyn still pitching smoothly, so far a no-hitter. There was another big crowd watching the game. Emilee saw Madelyn's parents in their usual spot, away from the rest of the spectators. Obviously, Madelyn's father was very pleased with his daughter's pitching. There was a broad smile on his bulldog face as he puffed a big round cigar. He was really enjoying himself.

A new spectator was in the stands this evening, sitting a few rows below the Taylors. A squat, round-faced, dark-eyed man with a clay pipe in his mouth, he was Isabella Lopez's father, watching his first softball game. He looked a little puzzled by it all, particularly the garish equipment his daughter wore behind the plate.

The Purple Panthers picked up another run when Sofia Hernandez got on base. She promptly stole second, sliding into the bag beautifully, drawing a big cheer from the crowd. Sofia scored on Isabella's ringing double to right center field. When the crowd yelled, Emilee noticed Isabella's father standing up, staring, the pipe in his hand, watching his daughter sprint around first. She slid into second with another beautiful hook slide, exactly the way Coach Wilson had taught her.

Mr. Lopez started to grin when he realized the crowd was cheering his daughter and he stood there proudly, very much pleased, but not quite certain about what had just happened.

In the fifth inning, the Diamond Divas came to life. Madelyn could not find the plate and the first two Diamond Divas walked to get on base. The third batter hit a ground ball down to third and Madison Moore fumbled it. Now the bases were loaded. It was the redhead's first error and it made her mad.

The Diamond Divas first baseman then slammed a ball against the fence in left field and three runners scored as Ashley Jones frantically chased the ball after it bounced from the fence. The score was tied 3 to 3 and the Diamond Divas were screaming happily in their dugout with a runner on third base. There were no outs.

Coach Wilson went out to talk with Madelyn. As she did so, Emilee, glancing towards the stands, saw Madelyn's father stand up with his jaw thrust out, hands on his hips, as if he were defying coach to take his daughter out of the game. Emilee wondered vaguely what he would do if coach did relieve Madelyn.

Madelyn continued pitching, however, and the Diamond Divas scored another run when one of Madelyn's curves got away from Isabella. The passed ball let the runner in and it made Isabella mad. She fired the ball back at Madelyn when she recovered it and young Taylor stared back at her, her jaw tight.

"Keep it up," Isabella snapped. "Keep it up with a runner on third."

The pitch had been low, bouncing in front of Isabella's mitt and spinning away from her. However, Isabella should have put her body in front of it, especially with a runner on base. That was a catcher's biggest responsibility with runners on base.

In the dugout, after the Diamond Divas were retired, the pitcher and the catcher had a few words about the pitch, and Emilee heard Madelyn say angrily,

"I can't put every one over the plate. What do you want?"

"Take it easy, gang," Coach Wilson called. "Everybody in here, we'll get that run back." It was 4 to 3 for the Diamond Divas now and it was still 4 to 3 in the bottom of the sixth when the Purple Panthers came to bat for the last time.

Jasmine Brown was to lead off and Emilee prayed she would duplicate her early home run and tie up the game. The tall Jasmine did not hit a home run, but she did hit a single right up the middle, the ball bouncing over second base and into center field.

With Hannah up next, then Madison and Isabella, the three big hitters in the Purple Panther batting order, the crowd started to yell again. Emilee wondered what coach would do now. With no one out the logical call was to bunt and advance the runner to second, giving Moore and Lopez the opportunity to bring her home and tie up the game. However, Hannah was the Purple Panther's slugger and you did not often call upon the number four hitter in a batting lineup, the clean up batter, for a bunt.

Sitting on the edge of the bench Emilee glanced down toward Coach Wilson. Coach was touching her hip, her chin, her right shoulder, her ear, back to her chin. The bunt was on because Hannah batted fourth and her spot was the right shoulder. Coach had definitely touched her right shoulder.

Emilee glanced at Hannah quickly, knowing that Hannah would not like that signal from coach. Hannah had not hit a home run this evening and she was anxious to get one. A home run would break up the ball game and give the Purple Panthers three straight wins.

Hannah had caught the signal because she touched her cap automatically in acknowledgment. Madison was out in the batter on-deck circle, kneeling on one knee and Isabella was picking her bat out of the bat rack. Things looked very good for the Purple Panthers and Emilee felt very good about that.

Hannah was to bunt on the second pitch and Jasmine Brown watched from first base, ready to break for second. The first pitch was in over the plate and Hannah took it for a called strike. It was the kind of pitch Hannah liked, a waist high fastball.

There was a little smile on Hannah's face as she stood up at the plate, waiting for the Diamond Diva pitcher. The pitcher put the ball in again, another waist high fastball, and Hannah, instead of squaring around to bunt, took a free, full swing.

With a solid "tunk" sound, the ball rocketed off the bat as if shot out of a cannon. It headed for the distant center field fence. The crowd stood up yelling. Purple Panther players tumbled out of the dugout, screaming as the ball passed out of sight over the fence, a home run and another Purple Panther win.

They gathered around Hannah as she came in after her home run trot around the bases. Everybody pounded her back. Even Emilee came up to slap her on the shoulder, but she felt a little queasy inside. Hannah's homer, her third, won the game for the Purple Panthers, but she had deliberately ignored the bunt signal given by the coach.

Emilee looked toward the dugout. The crowd was coming out on the field. Friends and relatives were swarming around the victorious Purple Panther players. Hannah's family was there, her father and two older brothers, grinning and laughing together. Mr. Taylor was speaking with his daughter, rubbing her shoulder, looking very pleased.

Coach Wilson stood alone in the dugout, smiling also, with her hands in her pockets. She had the hottest team in the Lake Forbing Little League with three straight wins, but Emilee Davis saw the troubled look in the tall woman's pale blue eyes.

When Hannah finally broke away from her family and came to the dugout to pick up her glove coach called to her. Emilee was standing close enough to hear the conversation.

The Purple Panther coach scratched her chin, looked across the field, and said slowly, "Did you see my signal Hannah, the signal to bunt?"

Hannah was unabashed. "Sure," she replied glibly. "But the ball was right over the plate. I thought I could drive it right up the middle and I did."

"You didn't miss the signal, then?" Coach asked softly.

"No, I didn't," Hannah said stiffly. "But the homer won the game, didn't it?"

Coach Wilson nodded. "We play the Pink Sox on Thursday night, Hannah. Do not wear your uniform to that game."

Hannah's green eyes bulged. "What?" she sputtered.

"You're suspended for one game," coach told her calmly, "for disobeying a signal."

She walked away leaving Hannah staring after her, open-mouthed.

"I hit a homer," Hannah sputtered, looking at Emilee. "I won the game!"

Emilee did not say anything.

"What a lousy coach," Hannah squealed. "What a lousy, rotten coach!"

"Everybody has to obey the signals," Emilee tried to tell her. "Coach is working for the good of the team."

"I'll quit the team," Hannah snarled. "I won't play anymore or I'll play for another team. That's what I'll do."

"You can't do that," Emilee said. "You can if coach decides to trade you."

"Then she'd better trade me," Hannah snapped, so angry there were tears in her eyes. "I hit a home run. I won the game!"

She could not get over that. She kept repeating it every time she spoke to one of the other players about the suspension, but Thursday evening when the Purple Panthers took the field against Melissa Williams' Pink Sox, Hannah Miller sat in the stands with one of her brothers, watching grimly. She was not in uniform and Maria Rodriguez was in right field taking her place.

Some of the Purple Panther players did not like it very much, either. Madison Moore said tersely,

"What's the matter with coach, anyway? Hannah's our best hitter and she won the game against the Diamond Divas."

"That's not the point," Emilee tried to tell her. "Suppose everybody on the club didn't obey the signals?

We'd have complete chaos on the field and suppose Hannah hadn't hit a home run and we'd lost that Diamond Diva game?"

"But, she did hit a home run," Madison Moore said. "That's what counts. Maybe coach shouldn't have given her the bunt signal to begin with."

Emilee shook her head in exasperation. "We can't look at it that way, Madison. You cannot have nine players on the field doing whatever they want, whenever they want. That would be total chaos."

"I would like to see a coach like Melissa Williams handling this team," Moore told her.

Emilee's lip tightened. "All right," she snapped. "The Pink Sox are in last place and we're in first. What does that look like?"

"It looks to me," Madison told her evenly, "that we're just good, regardless of who is coaching us."

Emilee looked at her hopelessly. In addition to all the other troubles they were having, the Purple Panthers were now letting their egos get in the way. Their heads were swelling!

She noticed that Sarah and Madison still did not talk to one another at all. Since the fight at the water cooler, each played as if the other did not exist. There was also a definite tension existing between Madison and Isabella. That, Emilee realized, might some day break out into a real nasty mess.

Destiny Johnson was on the pitching rubber for the Purple Panthers when they took the field against the Pink Sox. Sarah Anderson, leading off for the Purple Panthers, promptly slapped a single into left field on the first pitched ball and Emilee could see that Coach's time spent with the little shortstop was paying off. Sarah was coming around quickly.

Coach Wilson flashed the bunt signal from the dugout steps, touching her left hip as she went through a series of touching different locations on her body. Emilee acknowledged her and then bunted the second pitch down the third base line, nearly beating the throw to first.

Jasmine Brown flied out to right field. Then Isabella, hitting in Hannah's clean-up spot, slammed a hard single to center field. Sarah scored on a nice slide, beating the throw to the plate and the crowed yelled.

Again, Emilee saw Isabella' father in the stands, this time seated with two of his friends. The three of them grinned broadly when they realized that the cheers were for Isabella.

Then Madison scored Isabella with a long double to right-center field, bringing in the second Purple Panther run and Hannah, sitting in the bleacher seats, looked a little forlorn, realizing that the Purple Panthers could play and win without her.

The Purple Panthers scored three runs in the first inning, getting off to a nice lead. Destiny Johnson pitched good fastpitch softball for four innings, allowing three hits and one run. In the fifth inning, however, the roof fell in on Destiny and the Pink Sox kicked her around for four runs.

Coach had Samantha Smith warmed up in the bullpen and was able to relieve Destiny to stop the slaughter. Samantha got them out of the inning with no more pain, but there was plenty of damage. It was 5 to 3 for the Pink Sox now and the Purple Panther dugout was very quiet. The Pink Sox pitcher, after her bad start, had settled down and was moving along steadily.

Emilee nicked her for a sharp signal in the fifth inning, but could not get beyond second base. In the last inning, while it was still 5 to 3 for the Pink Sox, the grumbling started on the Purple Panther bench.

Madison Moore said, "We'd be ahead if Hannah was in the line-up."

Emilee realized the sense in her statement because Maria Rodriguez, who was filling in for Hannah, had no hits in three at bats, failing twice with runners in scoring position.

Coach Wilson was out talking with Hernandez before Sofia went up to bat at the start of the sixth and last inning.

Emilee said, "We're not whipped, yet. We pulled the Diamond Diva game out of the bag in the last inning and we will do the same with this one too."

"With Hannah in the lineup," Moore commented.

Isabella Lopez said from the other end of the bench, "How many coaches do we have on this team anyway?"

The redhead stood up and looked down at her. It was the first time Isabella had addressed her since the trouble at the park field. Moore said slowly, distinctly,

"Somebody ask you, Lopez?"

"I'm telling you," Isabella snapped, "Hannah got in trouble because she wanted to do her own thing. She got lucky and hit a home run. It was her own fault she disobeyed coach by not bunting. This team is not about what Hannah wants."

Emilee felt elated that someone besides herself was now supporting Coach Wilson, but the elation was short lived because she realized how close Moore and Lopez were to getting sassy.

Coach Wilson came back and neither player said another word on the subject, but something was purring and this purring could erupt into a vicious roar at anytime.

Sofia Hernandez dropped down a beautiful bunt and beat it out for a hit, giving the Purple Panthers a life in the last inning. It brought up the weak hitting Maria Rodriguez. Coach Wilson called time to substitute Madelyn in to pinch hit. With no bunt signal, Madelyn was clearly hitting away.

When Madison Moore saw that, Emilee heard her say tersely,

"She lets this girl hit away, but poor Hannah had to bunt. Why is that, because Taylor's rich?"

"That's silly," Emilee scowled. "We need two runs tonight. Against the Diamond Divas we only needed one."

Madelyn hit into a double play and then Sarah flied out to right field. The game was over and the Purple Panthers, for the very first time, felt what it was like to lose a Little League Softball game.

They walked off the field glumly with the cheers this time for the Pink Sox, who had played good softball and deserved the win.

Emilee walked with Madison Moore and Destiny Johnson, who was upset because the Pink Sox had knocked her out of the pitching circle. Up ahead of her she saw Isabella walking with Jasmine Brown and they were discussing the game.

Hannah had come over to join the team after the last out and she was walking with Madison Moore. From the expression on Hannah's face, Emilee could see she was selfishly pleased that the Purple Panthers had been unable to win without her. Emilee heard her say smugly to Moore as the two players walked by,

"What did you expect? You can't win games with a coach like that."

Isabella overheard the remark, also, and she turned around, her mouth hard. She said grimly, "You still crabbing, Hannah, because you were told to bunt and didn't?"

"Never mind," Hannah snapped.

"Maybe," Madison Moore said, "she has a right to crab. Maybe you would too, Lopez, if you had to sit on the bench."

"It was her own fault," Isabella snapped. "If we lost the game tonight because she wasn't playing, that was her fault too."

"No, it was Coach's fault," Hannah told her with a raised voice. "Don't you think I wanted to play ball?"

"Don't listen to her, Hannah," Madison Moore advised. "She's a dumb..."

The redhead never finished the sentence. Isabella leaped at her, throwing both hands and Moore fought back with relish. They were swinging and slapping at each other, grunting, with Emilee trying to get in between them when Coach Wilson walked up.

The tall coach stepped in between them and pulled them off each other. She was not smiling now and Emilee noticed that her mouth was tight. Coach said quietly,

"That's the last fight on this club, girls. The next time I catch anyone fighting, she will be suspended for five games. Remember that. Am I clear?"

The other Purple Panther players stood in a small circle, looking down, looking away. Isabella was rubbing her hands. Madison's nose was bleeding a little, but her green eyes were hard and cold.

They were outside the ball field and not many people had witnessed the quick exchange of blows, but a few had and had paused curiously. Coach Wilson went on slowly,

"Little League was organized to help kids your age learn about the great games of baseball and softball in an organized fashion. It is a fantastic organization and it is very important we keep it that way. It has a great reputation for good sportsmanship and clean play, with girls behaving like young women, boys behaving like young men, and all of us behaving like big leaguers. You girls didn't look like young women, let alone, big leaguers tonight."

They were all listening to her now and Emilee saw Madison look down at her shoes.

"Just like most teams, we've had our little troubles," coach went on slowly, "but this team of ours, I really believe, is special. We can go places if we stick together. I am doing the best I can. I know I may not be the best coach in the league and that most of you girls would have rather played with Melissa Williams' Pink Sox, but I cannot help that. All I can do is teach you what I know about this great game. Maybe Melissa knows a lot more. But, you girls will have to learn someday that when you commit to something, you have to commit completely, give it everything you've got and then give it some more, regardless of who you are playing or working for." She turned away and she said gruffly over her shoulder, "You girls better go home now."

She walked towards her old jalopy alone and then Emilee ran after her.

"Coach," Emilee called. "Coach!"

Coach Wilson turned around as she was opening the door of her car. "What's the matter, kid?" she asked.

"I'll play ball for you," Emilee choked, "and uh, and I'm glad I'm playing for you rather than Melissa Williams."

Coach Wilson looked down at her and then she looked away. It was getting dark now outside the ball field and Emilee could not see her face clearly.

"Emilee, I only got as high as what you might call a semi-pro ballclub. I was a catcher and I wish I could have gotten up to the big leagues like Melissa and starred in it, but it did not work out that way for me. I do not know why, maybe I just did not have it. I gave it everything I had, but it was not good enough. That is how it worked out for me, but I still love this game, Emilee. I would love to manage a club, a big club in organized softball, but if this is the best I can do, kid, then so be it. I am not going to regret it. However, I will promise you one thing. I will work just as hard with this Little League club as I would if I were managing a pro league club. You can count on it, Emilee."

"I know," Emilee nodded. "I know you will, coach."

Coach Wilson put a hand on her shoulder. She said softly, "Glad I got one little buddy on this club. Thanks a lot, Emilee. Maybe we will lick 'em anyway. They might try to keep one good woman down, but they can not ever keep two of us down."

"That's right," Emilee grinned. She was feeling better, already, even though she knew the Purple Panthers were troubled and a team in that condition seldom got anywhere.

## TOO MUCH FUN

The Purple Panthers went on a rampage after the Pink Sox defeat, winning five straight games, and pushing away from the pack in the American League. The regular season was more than half over and the league standings showed the Purple Panthers two and a half games ahead of the second place Diamond Divas, with eight games left.

The Lady Bandits in the Lake Forbing National League were far ahead of the other three clubs in the four-team league, undefeated in nine starts and looking to clinch their pennant soon.

With the regular season schedule winding down, the Purple Panthers prepared for another game against the second place Diamond Divas, who had won three straight and were not yet willing to concede the American League pennant to the Purple Panthers.

Coach Wilson started Maria Rodriguez against the Diamond Divas because Madelyn Taylor had a slightly sprained her ankle from tripping over a curb while texting on her smart phone. It was an ignorant mistake and embarrassed Madelyn. However, she was lucky she did not fall into the street into the middle of traffic.

Madison Moore said before the game got under way, "If we beat these girls once more we're practically in, and I feel pretty sure we will beat them."

"Let's not talk that way," Emilee warned her.

"All right," the redhead said, grinning. "We beat them twice already, didn't we?"

"Today's another day," Emilee observed, "and the Diamond Divas know they have to stop us if they want to stay in the race. Besides, have you ever heard of the revenge factor?"

"They have about as much chance of winning as they do stopping a freight train," Madison said. "We'll roll right over them."

In the first inning, they looked as if they were going to do just that. Hitting the Diamond Diva pitcher at will, they chalked up four runs, Jasmine Brown hitting a home run with a runner on base.

"That's it," Madison said, laughing as she raced out to third, the Diamond Divas coming in for their turn at bat.

The first Diamond Diva dropped a bunt down the third-base line, catching Madison sleeping. She grinned sheepishly as she picked up the ball after fumbling it a few times.

"She'll die there, Maria," she told the pitcher. "Don't worry about her."

The next Diamond Diva pushed a bunt down towards first base and both Jasmine Brown and Maria Rodriguez went after it. On a bunt to first, Emilee needed to race over from second to first and cover the bag for Jasmine, but Emilee, like Madison, was not paying attention either. Because first base was not covered, both runners were safe at first and second.

Maria Rodriguez looked at Coach Wilson on the bench and Emilee could see that Maria was worried. She walked the next batter to fill the bases and then the Diamond Diva clean-up batter doubled off the right field fence, scoring all three runners. She came in herself, on another single to right center field and the score was tied 4 to 4, with no outs and a runner on first.

Coach Wilson came out to talk with Maria Rodriguez while the Diamond Divas whooped it up in their dugout. Maria stayed in the game, worked hard on the next batter, and got her to hit a roller down to third.

Madison Moore stormed in fast to pick up the slow roller. This time, the ball bounced over her glove and went through her legs. The next batter hit a high fly to Hannah Miller and Hannah got under it like a big leaguer, and then lost the ball, which allowed the fifth run to cross the plate, putting the Diamond Divas in the lead.

It was 5 to 4 at the start of the second inning and Emilee could see the worry and concern on the faces of the Purple Panthers as they sat in the dugout. They had thought of themselves as unbeatable, yet the Diamond Divas were pushing them around as if they were the last-place Eagles.

The Purple Panthers went down in one-two-three order and in the Diamond Divas next half inning at bat, they chased Maria Rodriguez off the field with two hits and another error by Madison Moore. Madison let a hard grounder go through her legs with two runners on base and both runners scored, the batter going to third. It was now 7 to 4, the Diamond Divas on top. Destiny Johnson came in to pitch, but Destiny threw a home run ball to the Diamond Divas clean-up hitter and it was 9 to 4, just like that.

"Let's get started," Emilee called worriedly.

That was easier to say than do. The Diamond Diva pitcher was very effective after the first inning and the Purple Panthers had not gotten any runners past second base since.

It was 11 to 4 for the Diamond Divas in the fifth with only one inning remaining. Coach Wilson called for a big rally in the fifth, but it was the Diamond Divas who rallied, chasing four more runs across the plate, making the score 15 to 4 and it stood that way when the final Purple Panther out was made.

A soundly whipped Purple Panther squad left the field, none of them with anything to say. It was not a game lost because of bad breaks or because of a single misplay. The whole team had played poorly and the Diamond Divas had played well.

"One of those things," Coach Wilson said, trying to be cheerful about it. "We had a bad night. Next game we will do better. We are still in first place. Learn from the mistakes we made in this game, okay?"

Looking at the Purple Panther coach, Emilee had the peculiar feeling that coach was happy because of the loss. She did not say that, but it was in her body language.

"Every club has one bad game in its system," Coach Wilson said. "Now, we have gotten rid of ours."

On the way home with her father in the car, Emilee mentioned her observation and Mr. Davis said quietly,

"I wouldn't be surprised if Coach Wilson was glad you lost, Emilee."

"What?" Emilee gasped

"You girls were getting too arrogant and cocky," her Dad told her. "You were beginning to think nobody could beat you. Why even the best teams in the pro leagues lose many ball games over the course of a season? I think Coach Wilson realized your arrogance and cockiness and felt you were due for an adjustment. You will all play better ball next week. Just hide and watch."

"I hope so," Emilee muttered. "We really would like to go to the play offs. Can you imagine going to the championship finals, Dad, and playing in the Little League Softball World Series?"

"The Purple Panthers didn't look like a World Series contender this evening," her father said with a smile. "However, you do have a fine young team. I think you'll get back in stride pretty quickly."

They did get back in stride three days later, with Madelyn Taylor in the pitching circle against the lowly Eagles. A quiet, subdued, and grim Purple Panther team took the field. They made no errors all evening. It was the first time since the season opened that they played a perfect game in the field. They focused on one thing, winning the ballgame.

At bat they scored eight times as Madelyn shut out the Eagles with three hits for an 8 to 0 victory. They were still in first place. The following evening the Pink Sox stopped the Diamond Divas, helping the Purple Panthers consolidate their hold on the top rung in the standings. With two-thirds of the games played in their regular season schedule, the Purple Panthers now had a two game lead on the Diamond Divas and it seemed safe.

However, the Purple Panthers were not yet complete for they did not play together as a team should. Madison Moore and Isabella Lopez had nothing to do with each other. Lopez did not care for Madelyn Taylor, either. Madison had no use for Sarah Anderson, even though Sarah was developing into a very fine fielder and hitting consistently.

Hannah Miller was jealous of Jasmine Brown because Jasmine was challenging her for the league home run crown. Both girls had hit six home runs each as the end of the regular season approached. Then Hannah hit two home runs against the Pink Sox as the Purple Panthers soundly trounced Melissa Williams' team by a 12 to 3 score. Hannah clinched the title with another home run against the Diamond Divas in the final league game, giving her the home run championship and the Purple Panthers the Lake Forbing American league pennant.

Emilee asked Destiny Johnson the evening they won the pennant,

"How far do you think we will go, Destiny?"

Destiny shook her head. "Hard to say," she smiled. "We have to beat the Lady Bandits of the Lake Forbing National League to go to the district tournament and then to the section tournament and then the regional tournament…"

"Wait a minute," Emilee said. "Let's keep the Lady Bandits in mind first."

That same evening when they won the pennant, Coach Wilson had hesitatingly asked Emilee about her parents letting the team use their basement or patio for a pennant victory celebration the following night.

"My place isn't big enough," Coach Wilson explained. "Of course I'll bring all the party favors; you know the soda pops, the hamburgers, the ice cream, and cake. You think it will be alright?"

Emilee grinned. "My mom and dad already discussed it with me," she said. Then remembering Coach Wilson's old car and the kind of clothes coach wore she said, "Of course you're not supposed to bring or pay for anything, coach. I think most of the parents..."

Coach stopped Emilee right there, shaking her head vigorously. "My team," she stated. "This party is on me, Emilee."

The party was a huge success and all of the parents and players turned out for it with the exception of Madelyn Taylor's folks, who were out of town. Ashley Jones's father called upon coach for a speech as they were cutting the big cake and Coach Wilson said a few words, red-faced, fumbling, telling the parents what good kids they had and how she hoped they'd go far In the big tournament playoffs. She talked about their determination and the effect it had on their play.

While watching the tall, gaunt, homely woman she called coach, Emilee got emotional. She remembered how she felt after tryouts when she learned Coach Wilson had selected her to play for the Purple

Panthers, because Emilee had hoped, like everyone else, for Melissa Williams to be the coach.

Sarah Anderson's father, the tailor, was there. Mr. Hernandez, the Mexican restaurateur and Isabella Lopez's father, a banker, were laughing and talking it up. Jasmine Brown's father was sitting at the end of the couch, shy, aloof, but only briefly as Mr. Davis went over and spoke to him, breaking the ice, and making him feel right at home. You could tell both men were proud of their girls. The mothers were already planning another get together, this one without the men.

Mr. Hernandez, a short, chubby, shiny-faced man, made a speech, saying how wonderful it was that this Purple Panther team of kids was bringing together so many adults from all over town to an affair like this. He offered his sincere appreciation for the celebration.

Emilee watched Coach Wilson sitting in the corner, smiling, taking it all in. Coach Wilson, who did not have a family, evidently had found one here with this Little League team and she looked very happy.

# ANOTHER ROUND

The Lady Bandits, winners of the National League pennant in Lake Forbing won the toss for the single elimination play off game and took the field before a capacity crowd at their league park. Coach Wilson had Madelyn ready to pitch with Destiny Johnson available if Madelyn should weaken. One loss now would eliminate the Purple Panthers and coach intended to start her ace hurler every game, or whenever possible, until they reached the Little League Softball World Series or heaven forbid them and they lost.

The Purple Panthers started without any wasted time. Sarah Anderson grounded out, but Emilee doubled to right field on her first pitch. Jasmine Brown singled her to third and then the power side of the Purple Panther line-up literally blasted the Lady Bandit pitcher off the field.

Hannah tripled, Madison doubled, then Isabella followed with another double, and four runs were in. Yelling with the others in the dugout, Emilee saw the look of amazement on Coach Wilson's face. Even the Purple Panther coach had not imagined that much power in her batting line-up.

Madelyn pitched her usual smooth, consistent game and the final score was 11 to 1 for the Purple Panthers. The win advanced them to the district playoff tournament, the first small step on the long trail to the top. There were sixteen district winners playing for the district championship, with the winner advancing to the sectional tournament.

Emilee Davis tried not to think beyond the district championship, but she could not help herself. It was almost inconceivable that the Purple Panthers would get beyond the district playoffs, but it was there in the back of her mind all the time as they practiced and prepared to travel up to Mooringsport for the opening game.

Ashley Jones said to her that evening after the Lady Bandits win, "Think we have a chance, Emilee?"

Emilee nodded. "We have as good a chance of beating Mooringsport as they have of beating us."

"I didn't mean that," Madison muttered. 'I was thinking of the world championship, playing in that huge stadium for the Little League Softball World Series."

Emilee stared at her. "Do you know what that means?" she asked. "We can't lose a game. We've got to beat Mooringsport and we've got to beat everybody we come up against all the way to that final game."

"I know," Madison nodded. "I know."

"Stop talking about it," Emilee told her. "It's supposed to be bad luck to do that."

"I can think, can't I?" Madison chuckled. "I can dream, can't I?"

Emilee was dreaming too, realizing how wild the dream was. Any Little League Softball team, which reached the playoffs in the Little League Softball World Series Championship tournament, would have to be a great team, a real team pulling together as one, fighting like mad for every run, every pitch, bearing down every moment. The Purple Panthers were far from being that kind of team, not when four or five players were not even talking to each other.

Four busloads and several cars of players, friends, and parents went up to Mooringsport, thirty miles away, to witness the Mooringsport and Lake Forbing contest in the district playoff game. The Lake Forbing Little League Association chartered the bus the players were riding in. This was a Saturday afternoon game and as they drove up late Saturday morning, Coach Wilson looked as nervous as a mother hen with a dozen fluttering chicks scattered around a barnyard. The players could scarcely sit still in their seats and coach, sitting up front with the driver, kept calling back to them repeatedly,

"Okay gang, Take it easy. Relax back there."

Mooringsport, a city of over one hundred thousand people, was three times bigger than the town of Lake Forbing and the Mooringsport Little League Park facility was about twice the size of the Lake Forbing Park. The playing field, of course, was the same size as required by league rules, but there were at least two thousand Mooringsport fans in the stands when the two teams took the field.

The Mooringsport team had a left-hander pitching by the name of Jenny Kay Gipson, a tall, rangy, dark-haired girl, and Gipson could pitch. She struck out Sarah, and then she struck out Emilee. Jasmine Brown managed to hit a Texas league blooper for a single to right, but then Jenny Kay Gipson fanned the tough Hannah Miller to end the inning.

Isabella said to Emilee after Hannah fanned, "This is going to be a ball game. That lefty throws heat. Stay loose."

Madelyn started for the Purple Panthers with Destiny Johnson and Maria Rodriguez available from the bullpen. Madelyn was as good as ever, even against the Mooringsport sluggers. After three innings of play the score was tied 0 to 0 and Emilee noticed that Madelyn was really working hard, bearing down, and giving everything she had on every pitch, which meant she would tire in the late innings. Gipson, on the other hand, was working very smooth and easy. Her mechanics were excellent.

In the fourth however, the Mooringsport club broke the ice, reaching Madelyn for a walk and two hits, giving them a run and a 1 to 0 lead and it was obvious Madelyn was getting tired.

During that half inning, with one out and two Mooringsport runners on, Sarah and Emilee had broken up the incipient rally by pulling off a beautiful double play on a hard-hit ball over second. Sarah had to go behind the bag for the ball to field it, and then she flipped it to Emilee who whirled and tossed it to Jasmine Brown for the double play. The crowd gave them a big hand on the play and Coach Wilson slapped both of them on the back when they came in to the dugout for the top half of the fifth inning.

"We need to get that run back," Emilee said grimly. "Start us off, Madison."

Madison did start them off with a nice single over third. Coach flashed the bunt signal to Sofia Hernandez and Sofia dropped it beautifully down the first base line, pulling the first baseman in to field it, and Sofia beat the left-handed Gipson on the pitcher's banana run to the bag. Two Purple Panther runners were on with no outs.

Madelyn came up to hit, with Sarah on deck and Emilee in the hole. Madelyn, given the sign to bunt as well, placed the ball in a perfect spot in front of the plate, which advanced both runners, though the Mooringsport catcher threw Madelyn out at first base. It brought Sarah to the plate with one away and runners on first and third.

Sarah looked at Emilee in the batter on-deck circle as the left-hander threw four wide balls, intentionally walking Sarah and loading the bases for the force out anywhere. Coach Wilson came out to speak with Emilee and she said quietly,

"You've done this before, Emilee. This is just another ball game and it is not the last inning this time. We do have another at bat. So, just take it easy and hit the ball. We're going to score a few runs this inning."

Emilee just nodded, but there was a lump in her throat and she was breathing with difficulty. Her lungs felt compressed by an unknown weight. She had struck out once against Gipson and the second time she had rolled a weak grounder back to the pitcher. She had heard about this Jenny Kay Gipson girl, whose fastball supposedly clocked in at 62 miles per hour on a radar gun. From 40 feet away that was pure heat with no smoke, gas you would call it. She knew that she was batting against a good pitcher and she did not feel confident about being able to get a hit. Coach's words, however, made her feel better, so Emilee stepped out of the box, relaxed her shoulders, and took two deep breaths. She wanted to make good contact for the team, for Lake Forbing, and for Coach Wilson, who had never really gotten anywhere as a ball player, but who loved this game of softball and her new family of fastpitch softball players.

Jenny Kay Gipson pitched a curve ball, which broke right over the plate for a called strike. Emilee wet her lips with the tip of her tongue. She made eye contact with the three Purple Panther base runners and she could hear the yells of encouragement from the Purple Panther dugout. They had to win; they had to win every game from now on.

Gipson pitched again on the inside corner and Emilee's eyes lit up with an instant reaction. She swung her bat at the ball, driving the ball down the first base line. The Mooringsport first baseman lunged at it, missed, and the ball rattled down the right field line, fair by six inches.

Two runners came in and Emilee slid into second with a double. She got up, dusted herself off, and listened to the noise from the contingent of Lake Forbing fans rooting. It was for her. She saw Coach Wilson grinning, shaking a fist at her from the dugout steps. It felt good to be alive; it felt great to be a Little Leaguer playing to win a softball game.

They did not score another run that inning, but the score was now 2 to 1 for the Purple Panthers and everybody felt much better. There was talk, a lot of chatter, in the Purple Panther infield now.

In their bottom half of the fifth inning, the first Mooringsport batter singled to lead off. The next batter failed to drop a sacrifice bunt, and Isabella threw out the base runner who was trying to take second. Isabella threw the ball down with the force of a pro player and Emilee tagged the runner in plenty of time. Isabella had such a natural quick release of the softball for a Little League Softball catcher.

In the last inning, the bottom of the sixth, the Mooringsport team quickly threatened again. Madelyn was on her last legs, her curve ball was not breaking off as it had in the early innings and her control was not as sharp.

Coach Wilson had Destiny Johnson warming up in the bullpen at the start of the sixth. Madelyn had walked the first batter; the second had singled to right. With runners on first and second and no one out, the big Mooringsport crowd started to make some noise.

As Madelyn stood there, shoulders sagging, Coach Wilson walked out to the pitching circle, asking for timeout from the umpire. Emilee came in and she stood there listening to coach as she spoke. Madelyn's parents were in the sector behind the Purple Panther dugout and Emilee could see Madelyn's father, standing up, glaring at Coach Wilson. It was apparent he did not want the Purple Panther coach to take his daughter out of the game.

Coach said, "You're tired, aren't you, Madelyn?"

Madelyn nodded. She was looking at the ground.

"Arm hurt?" Coach Wilson asked.

"A little," Madelyn admitted.

"Okay," Coach Wilson said simply. "I'm putting Destiny in, Madelyn. I want you to understand they are not knocking you out of the game. You're tired and it's for the good of the team that I take you out."

Madelyn looked at her coach. To leave a game once she had started it was a new sensation for Madelyn. She did not like it too well, but she nodded, seeing the logic in Coach Wilson's statement.

Coach waved a hand to the bullpen and Destiny Johnson came in. Emilee saw Madelyn Taylor's father take a big half-smoked cigar from his mouth and throw it down angrily. He sat back down, arms crossed, his face literally glowering red with rage.

Destiny Johnson was nervous too, knowing she had to protect that slim one run lead. Emilee said to her neighborhood chum,

"You can do it Destiny. We're all behind you."

Destiny nodded gratefully. Coach Wilson said quietly,

"The infield plays back for the double play and remember we're in the lead. They have to make one run to tie us, two runs to beat us. Do you know how hard that is? Let them do the worrying. You, just relax out there."

Destiny Johnson pitched carefully and got the first girl on a pop-up to Madison Moore. The next batter, the Mooringsport cleanup hitter, slapped a hard, spinning grounder to second. Emilee fielded it, threw it to Sarah Anderson who was skipping over from short, and Sarah whipped the ball across to the tall Jasmine Brown at first. The throw was wide of the bag, but Jasmine stretched out completely and made a sensational catch, keeping her foot on the bag. The field umpire hesitated, and then she waved the runner out, ending the game. The Lake Forbing Purple Panthers were still in the tournament.

# SPLIT SEAMS

Two days after the win over Mooringsport Emilee heard the news of the trouble at the Lake Forbing Cotton Mills. She knew Coach Wilson had a job at the mills and had been there for a number of years.

Maria Rodriguez, whose father also worked in the mills, told Emilee about it.

"Coach was up for a promotion in her department," Maria explained. "Everybody thought she was surely going to be a superintendent, but another woman got the job and we all know why."

"What do you mean?" Emilee asked slowly.

"Mr. Taylor didn't like it that coach took Madelyn out of the game against Mooringsport," Maria said bluntly. "That was her way of getting back at coach. She could not fire coach because the union would not let her. That's how Mr. Taylor got around it."

"But," Emilee sputtered, "Madelyn was tired. She even knew herself that it was better she was relieved. Coach Wilson even told her why she had to take her out."

"I guess Madelyn's father didn't look at it that way," Maria growled. "He thought his precious daughter was knocked out of the game because coach did not leave her in. He probably felt that coach embarrassed Madelyn in front of thousands of people. Therefore, he retaliated by not giving coach the promotion she deserved and was supposed to get.

"Does Madelyn know about this?" Emilee asked.

"I haven't seen Madelyn since the Mooringsport game," Maria said, "but I'll bet she knows it and I'll bet she's glad."

"I don't believe it," Emilee said firmly. "Madelyn is not like that. She is a very compassionate person."

"I don't know what she's like," Maria said. "All I know is that coach was supposed to get that promotion and she didn't get it. Pop says all the people in her department are talking about it."

Emilee went immediately to coach's rooming house. It was nearly four-thirty in the afternoon and coach was due back from the plant in a few minutes. Emilee sat on the porch waiting for her, feeling a little sick about the whole business, knowing the effect it would have upon the team. Madelyn Taylor was their star pitcher and without Madelyn, they would go nowhere in the tournament. Now, many of the players might dislike Madelyn intensely and turn against her, thinking she had been behind the trouble at the mill.

Coach came down the sidewalk carrying her lunch cooler. As she eased up on the porch, she looked at Emilee and smiled, saying, "How goes it, captain. What's going on?"

Emilee was not sure how to begin. She finally blurted out, "Is it true, coach, that you didn't get a promotion at the mill because you took Madelyn out of the game against Mooringsport?"

Coach Wilson looked at Emilee and frowned. "Who's making that kind of talk up?" she asked quietly.

"It's, it's going around," Emilee scowled. "Is it true, coach?"

Coach Wilson touched her chin and then laughed. "Look kid," she said, "maybe a lot of people thought I was in line to be promoted and if they did, they thought wrong. Maybe this other person got the promotion because she is the better person for the job. I'm not upset about it."

"But it's wrong," Emilee protested. "If Mr. Taylor was behind it because you took his daughter out of the game that is wrong. Obviously, Madelyn had never been removed from the game before and Mr. Taylor didn't like it."

Coach laughed again. "As far as I'm concerned," she said, "Mr. Taylor doesn't even know I work at the mill. There are over two thousand men and women at that plant. I'm just one little woman in one small department."

""I want to talk to Madelyn about it," Emilee said.

Coach Wilson shook her head emphatically. "I don't want you to do that, Emilee," she said quickly. "Keep Madelyn out of it. If there is anything behind this crazy story, Madelyn had nothing to do with it. I'll personally guarantee that."

Emilee left after a while, promising that she would not speak to Madelyn about it, but she certainly did not feel very happy about the situation.

There was a practice session scheduled for the next evening with the second game of the district tournament to take place the following day. They had drawn Fillmore, a town sixty miles away.

Emilee arrived at the park practice field a little before five o'clock, walking down with Destiny Johnson.

As she crossed the street and entered the park, she saw a tight knot of Purple Panther players on the infield and then she heard the sounds. They were not pleasant at all.

"It's a catfight, Emilee," Destiny said quickly.

Her heart pumping, Emilee raced toward the scene. It had been a long time since any of the Purple Panther players had fought another, but there was a fight and they were throwing punches now. Emilee could now see the two girls in the middle of the group, pummeling each other.

"Isabella," Destiny Johnson panted.

Emilee thought at first that Isabella was fighting Madison Moore because of the issues between them, but when she pushed through the crowd of yelling girls, she saw that Isabella's opponent was Madelyn Taylor. Madelyn's nose was bleeding, but she seemed to be holding her own, giving as much as she got.

"Hold it!" Emilee yelled.

Destiny Johnson grabbed Madelyn and Emilee came up behind Isabella, holding her arms, pulling the two girls apart.

"All right," Isabella snarled. "Let me alone, Emilee."

"What's the matter?" Emilee asked her. "This is foolish, Isabella."

"It's not funny to our coach," Isabella snapped. "That girl's father gave her a dirty deal at the mill just because his prized daughter was taken out of a game."

"I have no idea what you are talking about," Madelyn flared. "I just heard about it here."

"You put her up to it," Isabella said bitterly. "You're a spoiled rotten brat and you can't take it."

Madelyn tried to break away from Destiny Johnson and throw a punch, but Madison Moore stepped in to help Destiny and they both held Madelyn firmly.

"There is coach now," Sofia Hernandez called. "Better break it up."

Emilee released Isabella as Destiny and Madison let Madelyn loose. Madelyn walked away, pinching her nose to stop the bleeding. Coach Wilson strolled up, her face expressionless. Emilee was positive she had seen some of the catfight from a distance, but she said nothing about it.

"Let's get going team," the Purple Panther coach said.

They held an easy practice session that included batting and bunting practice, drilling the infield with grounders and game situations, and plenty of fly balls to the outfield. Madelyn came over to Emilee after the infield session and she said slowly, "What's all this about, Emilee?"

Emilee explained the rumor going around while Madelyn listened, biting her lips.

"My father never tells me anything about his business," she said slowly when Emilee finished.

"I was sure of that," Emilee said heartily. I'm not blaming you even if it did happen that way, Madelyn."

"I'm going to speak to my father about this," Madelyn promised. "I'd rather not pitch anymore than have this happen.

"If you don't pitch," Emilee told her, "we'll never get beyond Fillmore tomorrow evening. Destiny Johnson is pretty good, but we need you, Madelyn, against these top teams."

Madelyn said slowly, "Coach told me she was starting me against Fillmore tomorrow. It doesn't look as if she's trying to get back at my father, does, it?"

"Coach isn't built that way," Emilee said.

"She has a right to, though," Madelyn murmured. "She should have been sore and she should have started Destiny Johnson out of spite."

"Coach wants to win," Emilee said. "That's all she thinks about and I'm sure she doesn't believe you were behind any of this business. She said she thinks this whole story is nonsense. Besides, being spiteful or vengeful is not who coach is."

"I don't believe it was a mistake," Madelyn said. "I, I'm really sorry about my father's decision, Emilee. I wished it had never happened."

At the end of the practice session as it was getting dark, coach called a halt. When the players came in from the field, she said quietly,

"Everybody sit down on."

The Purple Panther squad sat down, with Coach Wilson standing up in front of them. Emilee started to chew on the edge of her batting glove. She looked up at the Purple Panther coach outlined against the pink evening sky. Coach seemed very tall. She did not look so homely in the dim light. As Emilee stared at her, it appeared as if Coach's features had changed. She was still thin in the face with her carroty hair mussed a little, but the twilight skies made her look big and strong.

Coach Wilson said, "We've had a little more trouble on this team and I guess we all feel bad about it. I do not like it because this is a good team and it could go a long way in this tournament. I do not believe I have ever seen a more gifted and talented young girl's team anywhere. Each of you seems to have a natural ability to play this game, every one of you wants to learn how to get better, and I feel honored to have the privilege of coaching you."

The players were listening quietly, hardly moving on the turf.

"This is a good team," Coach went on, "but not a great team. However, you girls are so close to being one, a team that could go all the way and win this thing. We have pitching, we have fielding, and we have hitting. We do not have that one combination, though, which we really need to become a great team. We have no team spirit and we lack unity."

Emilee saw her put her hands in her pockets and look down at the ground.

"I don't know," she said almost helplessly. "I don't know what to do. Maybe it is my fault. Maybe it is because you are from so many different backgrounds that you think you cannot get along simply for that reason. There is nothing I can do about those wheels turning inside your heads. However, I can tell you one thing, and that is, we all bleed the same color. We can all, most certainly, get along."

She was speaking earnestly now, using her hands. "We have to recognize our troubles and try that much harder to work them out because each of you and I know what it means when we do. Winning this tournament is a pretty, big deal. We can get there and we will get there, but, only as a team of one, a team with one single mission. You must understand, the letter I is not in the word TEAM. Each one of you is going to have to give a little and take a little to get where we want to go as a team. Those wheels inside each of our heads must be spinning in the same direction or we are through. However, if we do come together, please understand you will never forget these moments in your life or forget one another for as long as you live."

No one made a sound. They sat on the grass in the park, their faces outlined from the evening light and then Emilee noticed the star, shining brightly, directly above Coach Wilson's head. It was a very big star, the evening star.

"There are a dozen of us here," coach said slowly, "and all of us are members of a Little League Softball team called the Lake Forbing Purple Panthers. Even though each one of you might come from a different part of town or lead a different life away from this team, when we come together on that field of play, we have to show the world that we do get along with each other, that we are a team of one that stands united together. Right here and right now is the place where we must prove that we are a team, that we are dedicated to each other for our team goal."

She shoved her hands in her back pockets and she looked down at the players for a moment in silence before going on. They could no longer see her face, but an outline, as the sky was getting dark while she stood with her back towards the remaining light.

"Maybe this softball team isn't important to you personally," coach said, "and maybe the name Little League Softball and the Little League Softball World Series Championship doesn't mean anything to you, either. If that is so, then we do not need to waste any more time, especially that of our fans, friends and relatives, who are really pulling for us, spending a lot of their time and their hard earned money to see us through to the end.

Coach paused and her voice became slightly emotional as she said, "If you girls want to win this thing, if you want to experience something you will never, ever forget, we will have to come together as one. We have to forget about who we are and focus on what we want our team to be. We have to be willing to help each other any way we can to get to that Little League Softball World Series Championship and it has to start right here, right now. You think long and hard about what you want and I will see you girls on the bus tomorrow. But remember one thing, there is no letter I in the word TEAM."

She turned and walked off into the shadows and the Purple Panther team sat on the grass, not one of them getting up. They just sat there, saying nothing. Then Emilee saw a cigar glowing in the shadows. A man had been standing there, a man with a cigar in his mouth, and Emilee realized that the man was J. C. Taylor, owner of the Lake Forbing Cotton Mills, the richest man in town. He had been listening as coach talked.

Emilee stood up, knowing that she had to say something as captain of the team, but there was nothing left to say. Coach Wilson had said it all or had she?

"Okay," Emilee muttered, "the team meeting is over. We'll meet at the bus station tomorrow afternoon for the ride down to Fillmore." Then Emilee did something she had never done before. She stuck her hand out, palm down, and shouted with glistening eyes,

"I'm in. Who's with me?"

Suddenly, as if a lightening bolt had hit the ground, the Purple Panther players all jumped up at once as one unit, trying to be the first to grab Emilee's hand. They formed a team huddle in doing so, jumping up and down. Then Isabella Lopez shouted out, "Let's go get 'em, girls, let's go get 'em." The rest of the Purple Panthers replied screaming the words slowly and in rhythm,

"Let's get 'ur done, let's get 'ur done, let's get 'ur done..."

They all shook hands and slapped each other on the back, then the conversation immediately turned to beating Fillmore. Laughing and yelling, some with eyes glistening, the Purple Panthers were ready to play ball right now. Tomorrow could not come soon enough.

Emilee walked home with Destiny Johnson and neither of them said anything until they were near Emilee's door, and then Destiny said slowly,

"You know something, Emilee?"

"What?" Emilee responded.

"That Coach Wilson," Destiny murmured, "she's a great woman, Emilee."

"I know," Emilee nodded. She had known that for quite some time.

Mrs. Davis was sitting up in the shadows on the porch when Emilee walked up the steps to her home, the newspaper on the floor next to her chair. Emilee heard the chair squeak a little and then her mother said,

"How did it go, Emilee?"

Emilee went over and sat down on the porch ledge, "I guess it was all right," she muttered.

"You've been worried the past few days," her Mom said quietly. "Get it off your mind, Emilee. Is it the team again?"

Emilee nodded and told her Mom about the catfight between Madelyn Taylor and Isabella Lopez and of coach not getting the promotion at work. However, when her talk turned to the team speech from coach, her face lit up and her Mom saw it.

"Things are never as bad as they seem, Emilee," her Mom told her. "You will see. You would never think a small softball team of girls could become so messy, but I suppose the drama with girls is so much like the drama with grown women. Your teammates have had their troubles, Emilee, but I simply see it as a team with growing pains. I believe you're going to work through these problems, your team is going to continue to mature and grow, and I really believe better things are ahead for you and that Purple Panther team of yours."

"Do you?" Emilee asked with wide, excited eyes.

"I think it'll all work out before you know it," her Mom assured her. "Just keep your pretty head up. Do not let anything discourage you. Always remember that if you want to see a rainbow, you must have a little rain."

"Okay," Emilee grinned. "I feel better already, Mom."

"That's my girl," her Mom said softly.

## MOVING FORWARD

Waiting at the bus station the next afternoon, her bag in her hand, Emilee learned from Maria Rodriguez that Coach Wilson had gotten a promotion at the mill.

"It's a better job than the one she was supposed to get," Maria bragged. "You think Madelyn spoke to her father?"

"I don't know," Emilee confessed. She knew definitely that Mr. Taylor had overheard Coach's talk to her team. Maybe Madelyn's dad must have reconsidered what he had done and then decided to provide coach with a better opportunity. Regardless, Emilee felt very good about it.

They went up to Fillmore and Madelyn shut out the Fillmore Redbirds, allowing one hit, and the Purple Panthers beat them by a 5 to 0 score. Hannah and Madison each hit home runs.

In this game, a silent, grim team took the field against Fillmore. Madelyn pitched the greatest game of her life and had a no-hitter going into the sixth inning. Even the Fillmore crowd cheered her on as she mowed down the batters.

The team gave her magnificent support all the way with no errors committed anywhere in the field. Isabella threw out the batter, who finally made the Redbird's lone hit in the sixth to break up Madelyn's no-hitter, at second base when she tried to steal.

The Purple Panthers returned to Lake Forbing with two victories in the district playoffs and now only four teams remained out of the sixteen original competitors.

On the way home, Destiny Johnson said to Emilee, "We're still in it, Emilee. We still have a chance."

Emilee nodded. They had a chance, but their prospects of reaching the finals seemed as far away as that distant star, which had shined above Coach Wilson's head when she gave her team speech.

Emilee did notice a difference, however, in the players. Madison no longer looked at Sarah with open contempt. They were not friendly, but there was a difference. Even Hannah did not boast about her home run on the way back to Lake Forbing after the game. Instead, Hannah bragged on Madelyn's magnificent pitching.

Isabella even complimented Madelyn by saying, "She pitched great softball. I've never seen her pitch better."

There was a difference, but it was still not the tightly, knit team coach wanted. The spirit was not there, but it was a lot better than it had been. Emilee now hoped that a team, with one of the finest girl pitchers in the country and with some truly fine hitters, might make it, even without the team spirit or unity Coach Wilson said they needed.

Four nights later, playing a tournament game on their own home field, they whipped a very good Blanchard team by a 4 to 2 score. Madelyn again came through with a fine performance.

This time it was Emilee and Sarah who led the attack, each with two hits, and it was Sarah's double in the sixth with two runners on that broke the game wide open, delivering the Purple Panthers the win.

Madison had been on base when Sarah came through with that clutch hit and Emilee saw the expression on the redhead's face as she crossed home plate with the final run. Moore had always questioned Sarah's nerve, but Sarah had proved with that ringing base hit that she could stand up with the best of them in the clutch.

They were in the finals of the district tournament now, with the town of Lake Forbing wild about its Little League team. The local paper was giving their games front-page coverage and the television sports news coverage was very positive. Bigger crowds were showing up, many from distant towns and cities to watch these finals.

The district final between Lake Forbing and Port City, played on Port City's field, drew double the crowd they had usually been getting. Coach Wilson, wishing to give the over-worked Madelyn Taylor a rest, started Destiny Johnson at pitcher, with Madelyn in the bullpen. Destiny surprised everyone by pitching a gem for five innings. In the sixth inning, Madelyn came in to relieve her with the score 3 to 1 for the Purple Panthers, two runs having come in on Jasmine Brown's tremendous home run over the center field fence in the fourth.

Madelyn put the Port City rally on ice and the Purple Panthers found themselves district champions, eligible to play in the sectional tournament. There were only eight section winners and that meant the Purple Panthers only had to win three more games to move into that coveted circle of teams that went to the regional tournament for the final play offs before the Little League Softball World Series.

A joy-crazed Purple Panther team returned to Lake Forbing after the Port City win. All the way back on the bus that night the girls were shouting, cheering.

"You know what this means?" Madison Moore whooped. "We'll be traveling on trains and planes now, playing in distant cities…."

"Until we're eliminated," Hannah pointed out. "It may be after the first game."

"Oh, no, we're not being eliminated," Madison cheered. "We're doing the eliminating. We're going to the World Series."

Emilee sat up in the front of the bus with Coach Wilson. It still did not seem possible to her they had come through as district champions and were now scheduled to play for the sectional championship. The Little League divided the United States into territories covering several states, also known as regions. A Little League team, therefore, had to win it's district, it's sectional, and then it's regional championship in order to earn the right to go to the host city for the Little League Softball World Series. Each year, a different city hosted the tournament. This year it was Libby Dell, Oregon, who everyone said was a beautiful place to play.

Coach was saying, "Mr. Taylor gave me permission to take off all the time I needed for these play-off games and the parents of all the girls have agreed to let them travel, so we are all set to go. Our paperwork is in order."

"You think we'll go all the way?" Emilee asked her.

Coach smiled. "We have a great pitcher in Madelyn Taylor," she said, "and a great team. We should go pretty far. Plus, we have the best team captain in the country." Emilee blushed and a pretty smile spread across her face.

The next two weeks were nightmares for Emilee. She could not remember what she ate or what she said, and she moved around the house in a dazed fog when the Purple Panthers were not playing or traveling to play other sectional winners.

They edged out a dazzling Pearl View team in the sixth inning when Sofia Hernandez came home with the score tied on a perfectly executed squeeze play by Sarah Anderson. Then they won a crazy game by an 11 to 10 score, with Destiny Johnson run out of the pitching circle early and Madelyn Taylor coming in to hold off the enemy until the final out. It was a very offensive game on both sides and the game came down to who had the last bat. Fortunately, it was the Purple Panthers, but oh, how close it was.

The sectional championship came around and it was another exciting ballgame. Madelyn pitched and allowed two hits and the Purple Panthers won by a 1 to 0 score. Isabella tripled in the sixth with Madison Moore on first and that represented the only run of the game. Now, just three more wins separated them from a trip to Libby Dell, Oregon.

"This is a solid softball team," Coach Wilson said with pride during a television interview after the close sectional championship win. "When we need hits we get them; when we need pitching, we get that too. You can't whip a club like that."

It seemed they would not be beat either. They went on to win the first game in the regional play off rather easily for a change by a score of 6 to 2.

Destiny Johnson said to Emilee after that win, "Do you realize we're only two games away from the Little League Softball World Series in Libby Dell, Oregon?"

"Keep your fingers crossed," Emilee laughed nervously.

It was true, though. If they beat two more teams, they would go to Libby Dell with the other regional winners in the United States and the International league to play in the Little League Softball World Series. It was almost inconceivable, but it was true.

Emilee could feel the increased tension as they prepared for the next ball game. They were all feeling it now; heightened from the excitement around them everywhere they went. More and more buses were traveling with the team when it left for out-of-town games; bigger crowds came to watch the home games and the crowds were so enthusiastic, making lots of noise.

The team had its picture in the paper with a few of the games receiving local television coverage. Mr. Taylor provided each player on the team with a new pair of softball shoes, each shoe having the latest molded cleat design. Sofia Hernandez claimed her new shoes were going to make her run even faster. Mr. Taylor also sent a dozen new bats for them. He offered to send a trainer to accompany the team, to keep them conditioned, and coach laughingly had to refuse. Even Coach Williams, the former pro league player, called Coach Wilson to let coach know she would help any way she could if coach needed it.

They nearly lost the next game, which would have broken the bubble and eliminated them from further play. It was another tight game and they were leading by a 2 to 1 score going into the last half of the sixth inning. Madelyn quickly disposed of the first two batters. With the bases empty and two away, the big Lake Forbing contingent that had accompanied the team started to make some noise.

Suddenly, an enemy batter lined a triple to deep left field and the tying run was on third base. Coach Wilson called for time and walked out to the pitching circle to talk with Madelyn.

After coach returned to the dugout, Madelyn threw one pitch to the next batter and the batter drove the ball deep into right field.

Emilee turned to watch it go, her heart sinking into her new shoes. The hard hit ball sailed toward the fence with Hannah Miller chasing it on her short muscular legs. Hannah had her back toward the infield and it seemed to Emilee that she was running faster than Sofia Hernandez could, the fastest runner on the team.

The opposing team was shrieking in the dugout as the ball started falling towards the low fence and then Hannah leaped, reaching up with one hand. The ball struck her glove, the tanned leather glove closed around the white ball, and then Hannah hit the fence, collapsing at the base of it with the ball still in the glove. The game was over.

The Purple Panthers carried Hannah from the field that afternoon, grinning, bruised, the happiest girl in America. Hannah yelled at Mr. Taylor, "Thank you for the shoes." Mr. Taylor leaned back laughing, pointing his glowing cigar stub at Hannah.

Winning their regional title a few days later needed to be anti-climatic. They needed a much easier victory than the first two games of the three that they had won to reach the regional play off final.

For the regional title game, Coach Wilson started Destiny Johnson and Destiny pitched steady, dependable fastpitch softball, allowing three runs. The Purple Panther bats were sizzling hot, driving in eight runs to give them an 8 to 4 victory.

Ashley Jones shouted as they were climbing into the bus still flushed with the victory, almost a little stunned at their success,

"We are on our way to Libby Dell, Oregon. We play in the Little League Softball World Series next week. Can you believe that?"

They were hardly able to accept the fact. Next week in Libby Dell, Oregon, the regional victors from the United States and the International league were going to meet in two separate brackets, Pool–A Division and Pool–B Division. This double elimination format was different, unlike any other tournament they had played in. Each team would play a minimum of five games with the two finalists playing for the Little League Softball

World Championship. Only five victories separated the Purple Panthers from the World championship. The ten finest Little League Softball teams in the world were going to play in Libby Dell, Oregon.

Emilee rode home in a daze. They had nearly a week to get ready for the finals and Coach Wilson worked them each evening at their home field, stressing the fundamentals, practicing bunting, base stealing. Sarah and Emilee worked for hours around second base, perfecting the double play. Coach stressed to them constantly of the importance at keeping runners off second base. They worked on several pick-off plays designed to catch runners off the bags, with Isabella or Madison giving the signals. By the end of the week, they felt better than ever, positive, and ready to play.

Madelyn was well rested and scheduled to pitch the first game. They had drawn a team from the West region for the opener of the series and as usual, the Lake Forbing buses rolled in filled with parents, relatives, and friends of the Purple Panthers.

On the way to Libby Dell, Emilee had the sick feeling that their luck could not hold out. It seemed almost impossible that a team could go on winning against opposition like this, but still one team had to do it, this one team eventually emerging from the tournament, champions of the Little League Softball World Series.

She sat with Coach Wilson part of the way on the bus and asked the Purple Panther coach, "You really think we have a chance, coach? There will be nine other teams down in Libby Dell, the best in this country and the world."

Coach shrugged. "They're as much worried about us as we are about them. Remember, we are regional champions too, and we had to fight just as hard to get here. They put their pants on the very same way we do, one leg at a time. However, every team needs a certain amount of good luck or good breaks, whatever you want to call it, to reach the top and to win this championship. I do not think we have used up our share yet."

The next day, as Emilee walked out on the beautiful Little League Softball World Series diamond with the other Purple Panther players, the crowd gave them all a big hand and she hoped that luck would remain with them. It was two hundred feet from home plate to the fences, yet it looked so much bigger. The park looked like it could hold 10,000 fans. This was unbelievable and so surreal. They had drawn the West regional champions from California for the opening game, the first pairing of the Pool-A division teams, and as Emilee watched the California girls working out on the field her hopes sank a little. They looked a lot bigger and moved effortlessly.

"The bigger they come," Hannah said succinctly, "the harder they fall." Both teams had their batting and fielding practice, and then the Lake Forbing Purple Panthers took the field with the San Hernando Dust Devils at bat. Madelyn Taylor picked up the new ball, rubbed it a little, and began her warm up pitches.

The first Dust Devil batter stepped up to the plate and the crowd roared. Madelyn threw and the Dust Devil slashed a single to left field. Emilee moved over to second to take the throw in and she saw the look on Sarah's face.

"*They're too big,*" Sarah was thinking. "*They're too good.*"

"Let's go," Emilee snapped. "Let's get two."

Madelyn kept the ball away from the second batter as she tried to bunt and the batter looped a foul into the air, which Isabella caught.

The next Dust Devil batter hit a rattling ground ball down to short that Sarah fielded, flipping it to Emilee covering second. Emilee's snap throw to first nailed the runner for a double play and they trotted in to the bench, the crowd giving them a big hand.

"Just like any other game," Coach Wilson grinned as they came into the dugout. "Ten players on each side and each team gets three outs an inning."

The Dust Devil pitcher was another tall girl, a right-hander with curly blond hair, and a tremendously fast pitcher. Like Jenny Kay Gipson, she consistently clocked pitches at 60 miles per hour, and from 40 feet away, it was the equivalent of a big league baseball pitcher throwing 91 miles per hour. She mowed down the Purple Panther batters for three innings until Isabella Lopez tagged her for a double in the fourth. Isabella advanced to third on Madison Moore's infield out, and then Coach Wilson signaled for the squeeze play with Sofia Hernandez, the team's best bunter, at the plate.

Isabella started in with the pitcher's first movement, barreling down the base path like a freight train. The Dust Devil coach yelled in alarm as the pitcher threw the ball. Sofia calmly poked her bat at the ball, bunting it out toward first, and Isabella was in with the first run of the Series.

The Dust Devils came back to tie it up in the fifth on two hits and an error by Sarah at short. Madelyn struck out two batters in a row to end the inning and the crowd gave her a standing ovation as she walked off the field to the dugout. The fans saw that Madelyn had not wilted under fire and Emilee saw the respect in Isabella's eyes after Madelyn struck out that second batter, bearing down with everything she had and then giving it a little extra.

"Let's get another run," Madelyn said quietly as she sat down in the dugout. "That's all they're getting off of me."

The Purple Panthers did not get the run until the sixth and last inning of the ball game. With two outs, the bases empty and the crowd beginning to anticipate an extra inning game, Madison blasted a ball over the left field fence and the Purple Panthers had made the first jump.

The team mobbed the green-eyed redhead as she stepped on home plate, grinning. It was 2 to 1 for the Purple Panthers.

Coach Wilson said in the dressing room, "That's one. There are only four other un-defeated regional champions left after today. After tomorrow there will be even less."

"Wonder who they'll be?" Sofia murmured.

"Who do you think?" Madison laughed. "The Purple Panthers and who cares who else."

They drew a team from the Central region in the second pairing and Coach Wilson selected Destiny Johnson as the starting pitcher. Destiny had come a long way since the opening of the Little League Softball season. She had gained confidence in herself and believed she could hold top-ranking Little League Softball teams. Coach Wilson had worked with her faithfully all during the season to help her develop control and poise when pitching.

This game was over quickly. The Purple Panther bats exploded for seven first inning runs and Destiny, with her comfortable lead, remained calm and relaxed, pitching a nice four-hit shutout. Emilee could not believe it. She pinched herself to make sure this was not a dream and she felt it. Three more games.

In their third pairing, they drew a team from the East region. Coach started Maria Rodriguez and for good reason. This line-up of the Maryland Clam Bakers players out of the East region had four left-handed hitters. It was a beautiful call as Maria worked with Isabella, inside and out, her fastball spot on and her big curve breaking across two planes. Hannah Miller and Jasmine Brown each had a home run and the Purple Panthers set the Clam Bakers down rather easily.

Now, the Purple Panthers could take a little time off and they needed it, especially the pitching staff. According to the rules, a pitcher could not pitch more than seven innings per day and if she did, she was required to rest one day. Any pitcher who pitched in three or more innings in a calendar day had to rest a minimum of one day. Studies had determined the pitch count and rest rules were reducing the risk of shoulder injury to Little League pitchers between ages eight to thirteen by fifty per cent. You certainly kept track of the pitch count because you did not want to risk injury or lose a game due to protest. Jasmine's mother had kept track faithfully all season long of the pitch counts for the Purple Panthers. After all, a team could lose a game from a later protest if they did not adhere to the pitch count rule.

Who would they play next Emilee wondered when she turned off the light in her hotel room? She knew the two teams playing for the right to play the Purple Panthers again were playing each other at that moment. Coach had imposed an early curfew and she did not want any of the players watching the game or even reading the newspapers. Her reasoning for shutting them in was to keep them focused. Emilee guessed coach was right again, after all, it was hard enough to focus without any added drama. "Which team will we draw," Emilee said silently as she dozed off to sleep.

The next morning the Purple Panthers heard during the team breakfast, they would be playing the team from Canada. Hannah promptly snorted, "We will just have to show those girls how good we are too." Of course, everyone understood because the Purple Panthers had not lost a game yet, that this team from Canada, who called themselves the Blue Jays, would have to beat the Purple Panthers just to stay in the tournament. Isabella said loudly, so all could hear her in perfect French, "avec nos lanceur et nos cogneurs, il juste ne va pas se produire!" She laughed at her teammates astonished eyes then translated for them, "With our pitchers and our hitters, it just is not going to happen."

Emilee realized at that moment this team had become one unit. The players were completely relaxed, yet spirited. Madison sat next to Sarah while Isabella sat between Madelyn and Hannah. They all could not wait to play ball again.

Coach chose to start Destiny Johnson again as the pitcher against the Blue Jays from Canada. Destiny had won once already in this tournament with a superbly pitched game. Could she do it again? In her first game, Destiny received a healthy supply of runs. Would the Purple Panthers be able to do that for her this game?

Destiny was nervous, however, at the start, walking the first two batters to face her. Two hits followed and the Blue Jays went up 2 to 0. Coach Wilson called for time and went out to speak to Destiny. Emilee trotted in also, and they discussed the matter rather calmly.

Coach said, "It's up to you, Destiny. If you think you can get them, go ahead."

Destiny Johnson looked at Emilee nervously. Out in the bullpen Maria Rodriguez and Samantha Smith were warming up. Emilee said quietly,

"Don't quit on us, Destiny."

Destiny bit her lips. "Okay," she murmured. "I'll get them, coach."

She continued to pitch, working herself out of the jam by giving up no more runs. A very grim and very determined Purple Panther squad came in to bat.

They got two runs immediately, Sarah and Emilee singling and Jasmine driving them in with a long double. They added another run in the third inning, giving them a 3 to 2 lead, with Destiny Johnson working nicely after the bad start. In the fourth, Hannah hit her second Series home run and the Purple Panthers had a comfortable 4 to 2 lead.

Destiny held the Blue Jays through the fifth and into the sixth and last inning. The two-run lead really felt good now. Once the sixth inning started, though, the Blue Jays came to life again. Two hits in quick succession put the tying runs on the bases.

Destiny Johnson got one batter to pop up to Isabella, but the following batter rifled a single to left, scoring one runner and making the score 4 to 3. There was another conference in the pitcher's circle, but Destiny was determined now, anxious to finish the battle. On the Purple Panther bench, Madelyn was yelling to her to stay in.

Coach Wilson said, "Okay, Destiny. You are the girl. We are behind you. Let's get 'ur done."

Destiny's face flushed and perspiration appeared as she toed the rubber to pitch to the next batter. With runners on first and third with one out Emilee hoped and prayed for a double-play ball, but Destiny struck out the next batter, making it two away.

The Purple Panther infield was talking it up, chattering, everybody behind the courageous right-hander as she prepared to face the last batter. The Canada Blue Jays team was on the dugout steps, calling for that big base hit which would tie up the ball game.

Destiny walked the batter after getting a three-two count on her. Now, with bases filled and two down, a contagious excitement moved quickly through the park.

Emilee had a look at Destiny Johnson's father in the seats behind the Purple Panther dugout. Mr. Johnson looked nervous. However, Destiny was not quitting. Gamely, she continued to fire the ball towards the plate, getting a strike on the batter, then another called strike on a beautiful curve ball. She had the batter in the hole with a 1-2 count. On her next pitch, the batter lifted a twisting ball toward short right field, along the foul line.

Emilee started for it. Jasmine Brown, playing first base, turned and sprinted after the ball. Hannah tore in from her right field position, her powerful legs pumping like pistons, her softball cap flying off her head.

The three players converged on the twisting, falling ball that appeared to be falling fair just inside the foul line. Emilee strained every muscle of her body, knowing the three runners on base had been running with contact and were sprinting round the bases for home with precious runs. Someone had to catch this ball.

She had a glimpse of Jasmine Brown, covering lots of ground with her longs legs, and then Emilee heard Jasmine yell loudly, "I got it. I got it. IT"S MINE..."

Coach had taught them to yell loudly for each fly ball to prevent dangerous collisions on the field. Emilee immediately pulled away and as she did so, she saw Hannah still driving in, eyes glued on the ball in the air. Hannah was not going to stop.

"Hannah!" Emilee screeched. "Nooooo!"

Hannah did not hear her. Hannah had not heard Jasmine's cry, either. There was a lot of noise in the park, everybody in the stands on their feet, screaming. Jasmine lunged desperately at the ball, clutching it in her first baseman's mitt, and then Hannah hit her on a dead run.

The impact was sickening, two bodies colliding at full speed. Both girls twisted repeatedly on the turf, Jasmine clinging to the ball as if it were a diamond. She lay there on the turf, almost unconscious, head rolling from side to side.

Hannah was moaning, rocking back and forth on her back, clutching her right leg. Jasmine had held the ball, however, and the game was over, another win for the Purple Panthers, but both players seemed to be badly hurt.

Emilee crouched beside Jasmine first. Her voice choked as she spoke, "Jasmine, Jasmine! Are you all right?"

The crowd was quiet, very quiet as the players and coaches came running over, gathering 'round them. The Para-medics arrived and after a brief examination of both girls, recommended they go to the local hospital for a more thorough examination. Jasmine was shaken up and incoherent from the collision while Hannah's right knee was hurting her so much that she could not walk on it.

Back at the hotel that evening where the team was staying, they waited for the news from the hospital. Coach Wilson had accompanied the two girls, along with their parents, and coach arrived just before dinner with the news.

"Fortunately, they are not badly hurt," the Purple Panther coach told the group of silent girls. "The doctors were afraid Jasmine might have a concussion at first, but she seems to be coming along fine." She will be okay after a few days rest. Hannah should be walking as good as ever after a week or so. Her knee is still swollen, but there is no cartilage damage. A bad sprain, that is all."

"That's great," Emilee managed to smile. "I'm so glad they were not seriously hurt."

"Of course," coach said, "they won't be playing in the finals. Hannah can't run and the physician refuses to let Jasmine play for some time."

Emilee stared at the Purple Panther coach and then at the rest of the girls in the room. Here they were on the eve of the Little League Softball World Series Championship game and the Purple Panther's were going to have to play without the services of two starters, their two home run hitters.

No one said anything for some time, each girl thinking her own thoughts; then little Sofia Hernandez put it into words for them,

"I don't care about them not playing," Sofia murmured. "I'm just glad they weren't seriously hurt."

# BLOWING UP

They drew the Asian Pacific regional winners from Beizhou, China called the Qiaohui (*pronounced chow we*) for the final game. The name Qiaohui, which means "skillful and wise," was apparently the perfect name for this group of girls. The Beizhou Qiaohui team was red-hot, having beaten their opponents by an average score of 14 to 2 to reach the championship game. They were reputed to be the heaviest hitting girls' team in the tournament, and after watching them take batting practice, Emilee was convinced that it was so. The balls seemed to jump off their bats, with every batter in their line-up able to hit the ball hard for distance. They were a confident team, knowing the Purple Panthers had been badly hurt with the injuries to two of their star players, Hannah Miller and Jasmine Brown.

Coach Wilson had to make hurried substitutions, putting Maria Rodriguez on first base and Samantha Smith in the outfield. Madelyn Taylor was the starting pitcher.

Jasmine Brown sat on the bench. She pleaded that she be able, at least, to put on her uniform and sit with the team during the game. Hannah Miller, also, sat on the bench, watching glumly, and when she got up, she gingerly limped around.

Coach Wilson had a conference with the players before they took the field. The Purple Panther coach said quietly,

"We have our work cut out for us this afternoon, no doubt about it. We have lost two of our best players and we are facing an outstanding team, one of the best Little League Softball teams in the world. Many people are counting us out already, but I know this team. You do not quit. That is why we are here. You have come a long way and you do not know how proud of you I am. Those girls put their pants on the same way you did this morning, one leg at a time. Now, go out there and play Purple Panther softball!"

Madelyn walked out to the pitchers circle, picked up the ball and looked at Isabella.

"Let's go," Isabella shouted.

The first Qiaohui batter lined a single to right field on the first pitch. The second batter doubled to left center, and the third bounced her hit off the center field fence, scoring both runners.

Coach Wilson waved her hands and came out to the circle, her face drawn. Madelyn seemed to be in a daze with the Qiaohui players hitting her as if they owned her. She stood there with the ball in her hands, the Qiaohui players whooping it up in the dugout.

"How is it, Madelyn?" Coach asked.

"I don't know," Madelyn muttered. "I just can't seem to get anybody out."

"It's a bad start, that is all," coach told her consolingly. "You'll settle down now. Just take a couple of deep breaths and relax before every pitch."

Madelyn looked at Emilee then at Madison Moore, who had trotted in from third base. Madison said tersely,

"Just keep firing that rock, Madelyn. We will get 'em."

Emilee looked at Madelyn, "We always have."

"You're arm alright?" Coach asked her.

"Feels good," Madelyn nodded. She had no excuses. The Qiaohui players had just hit her best pitches. It was just one of those things about this game of softball.

"A team gets like that once in a while," coach told her. "They'll hit everything you throw up and then, without telling you a thing, they'll stop hitting."

"I sure hope so," Madelyn murmured.

She was ready to pitch again and the next Qiaohui batter lifted a fly ball to right field. Samantha Smith, taking Hannah's place, danced around underneath it, looking very nervous, and somehow lost the ball. Another run scored and the batter went to second.

Emilee walked the ball to Madelyn whose face was gray now. This was the biggest game of their lives, and they looked as if they were falling apart when they should be playing their best softball.

The Little League Softball World Series Championship jitters were taking possession of them. After all these long weeks of tournament play, each game harder than the previous one, they were beginning to feel them.

Sarah let a ground ball go through her legs for another error and the fourth Qiaohui runner crossed the plate, still no one out. Emilee saw Coach Wilson in the dugout, her gaunt face very serious.

"We'll settle down, Madelyn. Do not let it get to you. This is just a bad start."

She knew deep down in her heart, though, that in a six-inning ball game you could not let a team get a big lead if you wanted to be in it at the finish. Right now, the Beizhou Qiaohui had a good lead.

The Purple Panthers were not particularly looking for a bunt now and the next Qiaohui bunter laid a beauty down the third base line, catching Madison Moore dozing.

The redhead lunged in very late, kicking the ball away and both runners were safe on first and second with no one out. The disappointed Lake Forbing crowd stared in amazement. This was not the team, which had clawed its way through all opposition, through the district and sectional titles, on to the regional, and through the Little League Softball World Series tournament to get here.

Even Emilee started to feel it now. A kind of panic swept through her, something she had not ever felt before in a game. She had been nervous at times, butterflies some would call it, but this was different. This was fear. She found herself hoping that a Qiaohui batter would not hit the ball in her direction.

They were playing back for the double play with Madelyn trying to keep the ball low so that the next Qiaohui batter would hit it into the dirt. Then she did just that and straight at Emilee Davis.

Emilee watched the ball bouncing and spinning towards her, a sharply hit ground ball, ideal for the double play. No problem, it was just a routine play for her. Out of the corner of her eye, she saw Sarah moving towards second to cover. The runner from first was streaking down towards second.

The ball bounced off the turf and onto the hard dirt of the infield. Emilee put her hands down the way she had done a thousand times before. She remembered to keep her glove relaxed on the ground, the way coach had taught her when handling ground balls, but something happened. Somehow, the ball went through her legs. She felt it brush her glove lightly and then horrified, she whirled to watch it roll rapidly out toward right center field with Sofia Hernandez sprinting in to recover it.

There was another big roar from the crowd as the fifth Qiaohui runner crossed the plate in this blowout. Coach Wilson called for time, her second of the inning.

She walked out onto the field, calling the whole infield to the circle. Emilee walked in, sick to her stomach, wishing she were back in Lake Forbing, wishing the Purple Panthers had not come this far in the tournament. It would have been better if eliminated in the first round of the district play off championship game than to come down here to Libby Dell, Oregon to play with such disgrace as they were doing here. This game, televised all over the world, was rapidly becoming a farce with no Qiaohui player out yet, five runs in, and two Qiaohui runners on base.

Coach Wilson looked at the infield when they came to her. Madison Moore, Sarah Anderson, Emilee Davis, and the first base substitute for Jasmine Brown, Maria Rodriguez.

"This is a bad one," coach said slowly. "This is a bad start. Right now is when the losers quit. You girls want to quit and go home now or do you want to finish this ball game?"

No one said anything. Coach Wilson went on softly, "This team has never quit on me before, and I don't expect it to quit now. I do not care if they score a thousand runs on you this inning. Stay in there. Give it everything you've got." She looked at every player in the circle, her eyes to their eyes, with a light grin.

Madelyn blurted out, "You still want me to pitch, coach?"

"I am going all the way with you this game, girl," coach told her. "Just keep throwing strikes and we will build some character."

Coach's eyes twinkled as she turned to go. Then she turned back around and said, "You girls remember the old story about the softball game with two teams playing and a girl asks them the score? Well, one kid says 24 to 0 and the girl says to the other team, 'aren't you girls worried?' 'No,' another kid replied, 'we haven't come up to bat, yet.'"

Madison Moore grinned a little, a slight, feeble grin. She turned and she said to Sarah,

"You miss another one, Sarah, and I will rub your face in the dirt. You hear me?"

Sarah managed to smile. There was no malice in the redhead's voice. These two girls had played side by side through many tough, grueling games. Moore had seen Sarah break up a ball game with a base hit to keep them in the tournament. Sarah had seen Moore's long home run clear the fence and win another game a few days before.

They went back to their positions now and Madelyn prepared to pitch. She worked the next Qiaohui batter to a 3-2 count and then the batter lifted a fluke single behind third, the ball barely cleared Madison Moore's outstretched glove.

Ashley Jones came in fast to field the ball, holding the runner at third, but the bases were loaded with no outs. Coach Wilson shook her head in exasperation. It seemed as if everything was working against the Purple Panthers this afternoon.

Madelyn took a deep breath, looked toward the bench, and prepared to pitch. The Qiaohui batter was rangy, long, and lithe, with a quick bat. She was one of their power hitters.

Madelyn quickly got two strikes on her. Emilee could see that she was beginning to settle down and she felt hopeful. Then the Qiaohui batter swung at the next pitch that was on the outside corner. A loud "tunk" sound told everyone in the park that her long bat had connected with it solidly. The ball flew out over Emilee's head toward center field. It was hit very hard, a line drive.

Emilee whirled to watch Sofia play the ball. Sofia was coming in very fast, running like a gazelle, but the ball was carrying further than Sofia realized. Emilee stared at her, seeing Sofia's mistake. That ball was still climbing yet Sofia thought it was falling!

Madison yelled from left field frantically at her friend Sofia, who pulled up sharply and began scrambling back. However, Sofia had already come in too far, too fast and the well-hit line drive sailed right over her head all the way to the fence. Sick at heart again, Emilee raced toward the outfield to take the cut-off throw. Madison ran over from her position like a deer to the ball as the Qiaohui players rounded the bases, the Qiaohui fans going crazy.

By the time Emilee caught the cut-off throw and whirled to fire to home plate, she saw the Qiaohui batter stepping on it, having made an inside the park home run with the bases loaded.

The score was now 9 to 0 for the Qiaohui and there were no outs. Emilee walked to the pitching circle with the ball. She handed it to the stricken Madelyn and she mumbled,

"All right, Madelyn, this is not your fault."

Madelyn did not say anything. She took the ball from Emilee's hand and Emilee walked back to her position. The excitement had died down and the crowd noise was mild. Breathless, laughing Qiaohui players sat in their dugout, confident the game was over.

Sofia Hernandez stood on the turf, deep in center field, looking very small, very still. Emilee did not know it, but Sofia was crying already, crying so badly that if another softball sailed in her direction she would not see it.

Isabella stood behind home plate, her mask under her arm. Isabella had done no wrong as of yet. Isabella was still the rock, her tanned face grim, unbeaten, talking it up.

"Let's go," Isabella roared. "Let's go. Let's go!"

Emilee considered there was no place to go. They were done, beaten by a better team, an infinitely better team. They had at last broken to pieces, this Purple Panther team of diverse backgrounds, this team that should not have even won the Lake Forbing league title with all of their troubles, jealousies, and anger, which had beset it. They should have cracked wide open a long time ago, but it had to happen now, before this huge crowd in the championship game and on live broadcast television for the world to see!

"Let's go," Isabella screamed, unfazed, this time from out in front of the plate. "Everybody, let's go."

Coach Wilson sat on the bench as stunned as any of the rest of them. She had not taken Madelyn from the game because she knew that if this team could hit Madelyn, they would destroy Maria Rodriguez or Samantha Smith. The bases were now empty and it was like the beginning of a new game. Emilee would have given her right arm if it could be that way again. That would be nice, to re-start the first inning and have the first Qiaohui batter come back up, with no outs, no hits, no errors, and no runs.

"Let's go," Isabella screeched. "Throw it to me, Madelyn. Throw it to me, you rich princess."

Madelyn looked at Isabella, the girl from across the railroad tracks, her battery mate. Isabella Lopez was not ridiculing her now. Isabella did not care about Madelyn's family money, her yacht, or summer home. Isabella only cared about one thing. She wanted Madelyn to pitch the ball, to bear down on these Qiaohui batters, because Isabella still had faith in her.

Madelyn got her first strikeout on three straight fastballs and her heater began to sing. Emilee watched her on the pitching rubber, the rich girl who had always had everything she wanted, but she could not buy this ball game, not with a billion dollars. She looked soundly whipped already, but Madelyn was not quitting because the poor girl from across the tracks, her battery mate, would not let her.

"Right here, moneybags," Isabella screamed. "Right here in this mitt. Make it pop."

Madelyn struck out the next batter with two beautifully breaking curve balls.

She got the third batter out on an easy roller back to her and then she walked slowly to the dugout, sat down on the bench, put her head down and the tears started flowing.

Emilee came in slowly. She saw Jasmine crying. Sarah sat down, looked at Madelyn and at Jasmine, and she started to shake a little. Sofia came in from center field, face tear-stained. She broke down completely when she came into the dugout and Coach Wilson had to grab her and hold her.

"My fault," Sofia wailed. "It's my entire fault. I lost the game. I cannot believe it. I lost the game."

"Shut up," Madison Moore quavered. "Shut up and take it like a champ."

It was contagious and it was moving through the Purple Panther dugout. Emilee felt the tears coming to her own eyes and she fought them back. The Purple Panthers had been in an iron band of tension for weeks that finally drew too tight and crushed them. They were like bundles of nerves, unable to control themselves. They felt licked too. Emilee could see that. Even if there had only been one run scored by the Qiaohui, instead of nine, that would not have mattered. They were licked. The Purple Panther's just did not have it anymore.

# WHY WE PLAY THE GAME

Emilee looked around the dugout. She wanted to say something, but she did not quite know what to say. She saw Isabella standing on the top step of the dugout with her kneepads and chest protector still on. She held her mask under her arm and her cap was on backwards. Her tanned brown face streaked with sweat and dirt because it was a hot afternoon and she had been working hard behind the plate.

Isabella snarled, "Crybabies! What are a lousy nine runs? We can make nine runs. Come on, play ball."

Coach Wilson was standing up also, smiling, confident. "That's the way to talk it up, Isabella. We are not done here yet. Everybody get a bat. Start hitting that ball."

Sarah stumbled out of the dugout and Emilee followed her, bats in their hands. Hannah called out to Emilee,

"Hit one for me, girl."

Emilee did not hit for her. The rangy Qiaohui left-hander had a snapping curve ball, a great riser, and plenty of movement on her softball. She struck out Sarah, Emilee rolled to third, and Madison popped up to short.

The Qiaohui pitcher was very good and with a nine run cushioned lead, she did not really have to be. Emilee tried to hope something positive was going to happen, but it was very difficult. Nine runs were still nine runs no matter how mad Isabella Lopez got and she remembered Jasmine and Hannah were out of the line-up, with two weak hitters replacing them.

"We'll get 'em," Isabella snapped as she went out to start the second inning.

Madelyn seemed to have found her stride in the second inning and she set the Qiaohui down in one-two-three order. Not one of the Qiaohui got the ball out of the infield this time around. Emilee came up with a nice play on a ground ball and the Lake Forbing crowd had a little something to cheer. It was not much though, not with that big number 9 followed by a big number 0 on the scoreboard.

Isabella led off the bottom of the second, batting in the clean-up spot with Hannah on the bench and she created a little excitement when she ripped a triple down the left field line. Her headfirst slide into third beat the throw from the outfield.

"That's our start," Coach Wilson yelled. "Everybody hits now."

Madison scored Isabella with a sacrifice fly to center field and the Purple Panthers were on the scoreboard with one run. Madelyn then hammered a double to right and scored on Sarah's single up the middle. She hit the dirt in another flying, headfirst dive at home plate. It duplicated Isabella's slide into third.

Isabella helped Madelyn to her feet and pounded her back after Madelyn scored that run. Emilee, waiting to bat, heard her say,

"You slide like a girl from my side of town, Madelyn. Nice goin'!"

"Si," Madelyn grinned. "Si, senorita."

Emilee sent Sarah to third on another single to right and the Lake Forbing crowd started to make some noise. The Purple Panthers were scratching away at that rangy left-hander and they were scoring runs.

Madison hit a hard shot over second, moving Emilee to third and scoring Sarah. It was now 9 to 3 for the Qiaohui who suddenly did not seem to be so sure themselves. The big crowd watching the Little League Softball World Series was getting a bit more interested too. Was the momentum shifting?

Sofia Hernandez looked at Coach Wilson prior to stepping into the box. Coach hesitated a moment and then gave the sign for Sofia to bunt. Emilee grasped the strategy immediately. The Qiaohui players were not looking for a sacrifice bunt from a team six runs down and Sofia was definitely a good bunter and very fast.

Sofia dropped the ball down the third base line, catching the Qiaohui third baseman asleep. Emilee held at third and the bases were now loaded with one out.

The Lake Forbing crowd started to whoop it up again. They were a small, but noisy, delegation at this big Libby Dell, Oregon field and they were making themselves heard. The weak part of the Purple Panther batting order was coming up, in Maria Rodriguez and Samantha Smith. Maria almost upset the applecart by sending a line drive straight at the third baseman, which, if it had gotten by her, would have gone for two bases. She was out, however, and Samantha stepped into the batter's box.

On her very first pitch to Samantha, the Qiaohui left-hander grazed Smith on the thigh. Emilee walked home for the fourth run of the inning. The bases were still loaded, but the Purple Panthers also had two outs.

It brought Isabella up and the Purple Panthers needed some more runs badly. The entire Purple Panther team was out on the dugout steps offering encouragement, as she stood there at the plate, very quiet, hardly moving her bat, eyeing the opposing pitcher.

Isabella hit another hard liner, which the center fielder fielded on one bounce. Madison scored easily but Sofia held at third. The score was 9 to 5 and the Purple Panthers were back in the ball game. The Beizhou coach, however, relieved the Qiaohui left-hander, with a short, muscular right-hander coming in to take her place.

They were going crazy in the Purple Panther dugout. Sarah was up, with Emilee on deck. Madelyn was yelling happily at Isabella on first base. Madison was whooping, "Come on, Sarah! Come on, Sarah."

Emilee, in the on-deck circle, turned her head to look at Madison. She remembered the many days Madison looked upon Sarah with contempt and when Isabella could stand Madelyn. Here in this final game of the series, beaten and battered by this great Qiaohui team in the first inning, they were finding themselves. The team Coach Wilson had always wanted she now had, finally. Was it soon enough?

The umpire allowed the new pitcher to take her warm-up pitches and signaled Sarah to the plate. The shortstop watched one pitch for a called strike and then swung at the second, slicing it out toward left field, another line drive, certainly another base hit.

The Purple Panther runners were racing around the bases on contact when the Qiaohui left fielder took a flying dive toward the ball, spearing it inches off the turf for the third and final out of the inning.

Sarah looked as if she were going to cry when she trotted out to her position and Madison Moore called over to her encouragingly, "Shake it off. You couldn't come any closer than that, Sarah."

Madelyn retired the Qiaohui batters in order, two more strikeouts, and a slow roller out to Sarah. The Qiaohui right-hander followed suit with the Purple Panthers, with one strikeout and two infield outs.

Again, Madelyn took the pitching rubber and again, Madelyn sent three Qiaohui batters back to the dugout with three straight strikeouts and Emilee realized that Madelyn had pitched no hit-ball for four innings after the initial nine runs scored. Those heavy Qiaohui bats were completely silent now. They were not even getting a loud foul off Madelyn. Her pitching was beautiful.

At the end of the inning when Madelyn came in, Isabella waited for her on the foul line and they walked to the dugout together, Isabella grinning with one hand on Madelyn's shoulder.

"She's good," Isabella screeched in the dugout. "This girl is great. Have you ever seen her pitches move like that? She is throwing gas."

Emilee led off the bottom of the fourth. Her mother and father were watching from the stands and she was using the bat her father had helped her purchase at the start of the season. It was a good bat and her father was yelling, wanting her to do something with it. She did by slashing a single over first on the very first pitch and the Purple Panthers had new life.

They needed only four runs to tie the game up and those four runs did not look so big anymore. They proof this afternoon was they could play when down, that they would play until the game ended. Now, the Qiaohui players worried and fought the jitters.

Madison Moore dropped another single into right field and the frantic Qiaohui coach immediately yanked her right-hander and brought in another left-hander to stop these persistent Purple Panther bats.

It was Lopez, Davis, and Hernandez in order now, and Emilee was positive they were going to do something no matter who pitched for the Qiaohui. Lopez was up waiting, swinging two bats, looking out at the new pitcher warming up, looking at the two runners on the bases. Lopez had started all of this off and Emilee just knew Isabella was not going to fail now.

Hannah boomed from the bench, "Come on, Isabella! Come on!"

Isabella sent a torrid line drive into the gap between the right and center fielders. Emilee was off with the crack of the bat, scoring easily, with Madison Moore pounding the plate behind her. Isabella pulled up at second with a double and the score was 9 to 7 for the Qiaohui.

The Lake Forbing crowd was acting crazy now as Madison Moore came up with no outs and a runner on second. Madison hit a long fly ball to center field and the Qiaohui center fielder pulled it in for the first out, with Isabella remaining on second.

Sofia faked another bunt and then looped a single to left field. Isabella made a perfect turn at third base and pounded down the base path towards home. Again, with the Lake Forbing players howling, Isabella went into the plate with another flying, headfirst slide, but this time she was a fraction of a second too late. The Qiaohui outfielder made a beautiful throw to the plate and the catcher was able to tag Isabella' shoulder as she came in. The umpire waved her out.

Sofia skipped down to second on the throw and it was two away with Maria Rodriguez batting, the score still 9 to 7 for the Qiaohuis.

They begged Maria to come through with a hit and Maria almost made it. Her line shot down the right field line landed foul by about six inches. It would surely have been a double if it had stayed in.

On the next pitch, Maria made the third out on a ground ball to second and the side was retired. The Qiaohui came off the field to start the fifth inning. Emilee trotted out to second base, wondering if they would make it. They had come so far, but two big runs separated them from the Qiaohui lead. She knew with only two innings remaining those runs could be very hard to get.

Madelyn was really pitching though, throwing her beautiful curve ball while mixing it up with fastballs, risers, and change-ups the way Coach Wilson had taught her to. The Qiaohui batters could no longer hit her softball. Madelyn was masterfully manipulating their timing. That had always been her key, her ability to throw off the opposing batters' timing. Again, they went down in order, a strikeout, and an easy fly to Sofia, and then a slow roller to Emilee. Madelyn had set down fifteen straight batters without a hit, without even one Qiaohui batter reaching first base.

The crowd realized it and gave her an ovation as she walked off the field towards the dugout. They knew what it had taken out of the Purple Panther pitcher to settle down after a team had scored nine runs off her in one inning.

Emilee noticed that Isabella sat with Madelyn on the bench now. They discussed the Qiaohui batters between innings. They were real battery mates in every sense of the word. It was no longer Madelyn Taylor from River Oaks and Isabella Lopez from the tenement housing project on the other side of the tracks. They were Taylor and Lopez, the battery mates for the Lake Forbing Purple Panthers.

"Two runs," Coach Wilson said. "We need two more, gang. Let's put it on ice now."

Samantha Smith went down with an infield fly and it was one away with Madelyn coming up to bat. The big Series crowd gave Madelyn a big round of applause again, and she reddened a little as she walked to the plate to bat.

Sarah was on deck, with Emilee following her. All of the Purple Panthers had been swinging a good bat so far in the game.

Madelyn started the ball rolling again. The Purple Panther pitcher ripped a line drive single out to center field. The Purple Panther players started to yell as Sarah came up to the plate, and Sarah responded with another single to left field, sending Madelyn to second.

Knowing the Purple Panthers needed another hit, Emilee came up to the plate resolved to do just that. The new Qiaohui left-hander had a nice curve ball and she broke the first pitch right over the plate. Emilee waited for another, looking for a pitch in her zone, one she could really pop. With a 1-1 count, she got it and hit the pitch right back up the middle for another single. This was the third single in a row for the Purple Panthers. Madelyn did not try to score on the hit because the center fielder fielded it quickly and she had great throwing arm, a real cannon.

The bases were filled with the always-tough Madison Moore in the batters box and Isabella Lopez on deck. There was a long conference between the Qiaohui coach and players in the pitching circle. Moore just stood there to one side of the plate, watching them, not smiling.

Emilee watched her from first base. She saw Isabella talking to her, and she remembered the days when Isabella and Madison had got after one another at the ball field. Those days were behind them now.

They were going to leave the left-hander in the game and Emilee suspected it was because the Beizhou Qiaohui did not have any other good pitchers, the Purple Panthers having pummeled every one of them.

Madison Moore stepped up to the plate, waved her bat at the Qiaohui pitcher, and waited for the delivery. The Qiaohui infield was playing back for the double play at second with one away.

The big series crowd was literally bubbling over with excitement. The fathers of the Purple Panther players were all hoarse from shouting. J. C. Taylor sat with Luis Lopez and Mr. Davis the electrician. They were all leaning forward, sweating it out. Madison Moore's dad was a few seats away, yelling at his daughter, shaking his fist.

The green-eyed redhead appeared a lot calmer than her father did. She stood there at the plate, her bat on her shoulder, waiting for the pitch. The Qiaohui left-hander wound up and delivered her a curve on the outside corner. Madison fouled off the second pitch, which put her in a hole with the count now 0-2, no balls and two strikes.

The redhead remained calm. With confident coolness, she watched the Qiaohui pitcher, taking a ball and then another ball. On the 2-2 pitch, she swung at a curve and connected with it solidly, driving it down the third base line.

The Qiaohui third baseman lunged at it and the ball skipped off her glove and rolled down the line towards the left field corner. Madelyn tore in from third with one run; Sarah streaked down the path and crossed over home plate in a blur with the tying run.

The stadium went wild. Pandemonium broke out in the Lake Forbing dugout. Everybody was standing up, screaming. Madison Moore stood on first base, grinning.

Hannah Miller, bad leg and in pain, did a war dance in front of the Purple Panther dugout.

Coach Wilson just stood there; scarcely able to believe they had tied up the game after being nine runs down. Even the umpires out on the field were shaking their heads in amazement and admiration.

This time the Qiaohui coach removed the left-hander from the game and another Qiaohui pitcher took over, this one a right-hander. It was one away with runners on first and second, Isabella batting with a hot bat for a new pitcher to face. Isabella was on fire and she was not stopping now with victory in their grasp.

The excitement died down a little as the Qiaohui pitcher took her warm-up pitches and then, she was ready to go. Emilee waited on second. She watched Isabella adjust her batting helmet and take her familiar, widespread stance at the plate.

The Qiaohui pitcher pitched the ball and Isabella drove another line drive out to right field. Emilee took off with the crack of the bat, knowing this might be the winning run of the ball game. As she streaked toward third, she saw her third base coach waving her on, and she drove off the inside corner of the bag with her left foot, legging it for home.

She saw the faces of the Purple Panther players as they tumbled out of the dugout, screaming as she ran. The Qiaohui catcher was waiting for the throw-in, very tense, glove raised. It was going to be close, very close.

Ten feet from the plate, Emilee stretched out into a long, headfirst slide. She went in on her stomach, reaching for the plate with her hands, scraping past the Qiaohui catcher. When her fingers finally contacted the smooth rubber surface of the plate, she felt the ball being jammed into the middle of her back.

She heard the howl of joy then, from the Purple Panther dugout, and she looked up to see the umpire crouching above her, both hands down, palms flattened toward the ground. "Safe," the umpire boomed. The score was 10 to 9; the Purple Panthers were in the lead.

The Purple Panther players came out to pick Emilee up, carry her off the field and into the dugout, sweaty, dusty, breathless, but smiling beautifully. A glum Qiaohui team waited on the field for the game to continue. There were runners on second and third with only one out.

They intentionally walked Madison Moore, filling the bases, hoping for the double play. They succeeded with Sofia hitting back to the pitcher. The pitcher threw the ball to home and the catcher whipped it to first just ahead of the fast Hernandez. The inning was over, the Purple Panthers led by one run and Madelyn had not given up a hit or a walk since that bad first inning. It was the sixth and last inning now with only three outs standing between the Purple Panthers and the Little League Softball World Series Championship.

They raced out onto the field, confident of victory now. They were a team who could not be beat, would not be beat, with the greatest girl softball pitcher in the world pitching from the pitching circle.

Madelyn was very calm, very relaxed, pitching carefully, steadily.

She got the first Qiaohui batter on a roller down to Moore. She worked slowly on the next batter, working her to a full count of 3-2, and then striking her out with a nasty curve.

The entire crowd was standing up now with two out in this last inning of the game, no runners on the bases, and the game practically over. Coach Wilson kept calling from the dugout,

"Take it easy gang; very easy out there."

She was as nervous as the players were and she had not sat down since the first inning.

Madelyn pitched to the Qiaohui catcher, getting two strikes on her. Emilee stood at second, her hands sweating, head whirling, waiting. One more strike, one more out, and they were in.

Madelyn was not going to give that next batter anything to drive. She worked very slowly. The batter fouled off two pitches. The batter pushed the count to 3-2, and then fouled off two more pitches, with everybody on the field and in the stands on edge.

The next pitch was inside and Madelyn thought it was good, as did Emilee who opened her mouth to scream. However, the umpire called ball, sending the batter down to first base, the first Qiaohui runner to reach a base since the first inning.

Madelyn did not like it but she was not going to argue with an umpire. Emilee could see that Coach Wilson did not like it either, thinking the last pitch was a strike, but coach did not come out of the dugout.

They were not arguing with umpires this afternoon, knowing the man behind the plate was calling them just as he saw them, but they still thought the ball had been a strike.

The tying run was on first and the game was not over. Emilee felt the tension coming back even now, with two outs and Madelyn pitching beautifully.

The Qiaohuis took their pitcher out of the game and put in a pinch hitter to bat for her. The pinch hitter rubbed dirt on her bat and stepped up to the plate with a very determined look.

She swung at the first pitch, hitting it out towards right field where Samantha Smith was playing in Hannah's place. When Emilee saw the ball sailing out that way, she suddenly stopped breathing. The ball was well hit and carrying quickly towards the fence.

Samantha backed up for it. She backed all the way to the fence, nervous, moving from one side to the other. She was right back against the low fence now, reaching up for the ball.

Then it happened and it was a softball freak play if there ever was one. No one could believe what he or she saw. The ball struck the palm of Samantha's glove, bounced out of it and over the fence.

For a very long moment, there was absolutely no sound on the field. Then, the big Qiaohui crowd came alive. A girl in the Qiaohui dugout was screaming insanely. The Qiaohui batter was rounding first, going towards second, and Emilee watched her pulling up, slowing into her home run trot as she realized she had just hit one. This pinch hitter had just given the Qiaohui the lead again at 11 to 10.

It did not make sense and it was not fair. It was a trick played on the Purple Panthers, somehow, by an unknown evil softball spirit. The ball had bounced out of the glove and then had passed over the fence without touching the ground. Therefore, it was a home run.

Samantha stood there, staring toward home plate, shoulders drooping, her glove at her side as the two runners crossed home plate. The Lake Forbing crowd watched, stupefied, unable to accept the fact this amazing come from behind victory was no longer in their hands.

Madelyn went on pitching, still very cool, unperturbed. She struck out the final Qiaohui batter and the Purple Panthers ran in for the last bat of the sixth and final inning.

Madelyn waited at the top of the dugout for Samantha to come in and Samantha looked sick as she crossed the infield from right field. She was crying too, the way Sofia Hernandez had cried, and her hands were twitching. Madelyn gave her a friendly slap on the shoulder as Madelyn went down into the dugout to show her that there were no hard feelings because of her disastrous and freaky error.

Samantha sat down with her face in her hands. She was shaking convulsively and Coach Wilson sat down next to her, talking to her calmly.

Coach called every one around and while looking at each of them with a big grin she said,

"In case any of you ever wondered, this is why we play the game. Is this the most exciting game you have ever played in, the most exciting time of your life? Huh?

Now, it is our turn to bat and I do believe in you. So, let's get 'ur done!"

Maria Rodriguez was up to hit and Samantha was to bat second, but everyone could see she was in no condition to do that. She was not herself and it would be a while before she calmed down.

The Purple Panthers were one run behind with the bottom of their lineup coming to bat. Could they pull off another miracle? It hardly seemed possible. That fluke home run had been a crushing blow, a knockdown, one that might keep them down. Was that their destiny? Their coach did not think so.

Rodriguez was determined, but she flied to left field for the first out. Emilee was on the dugout steps with the others and she turned to see what Coach Wilson would do about Samantha. Then she saw the injured Hannah Miller standing in front of coach, talking rapidly. Hannah had her favorite bat in her hands and it was apparent Hannah wanted to bat for Samantha.

Remembering some of Hannah's long home runs in the past, Emilee felt her hopes rise a little. Hannah could not run, but if she hit one over the fence, she would not have to. She could crawl around the bases to tie the score again.

Coach Wilson finally gave her consent to Hannah to bat and the girl hobbled out of the dugout, walking painfully with a bad limp to home plate. The crowd gave her a standing ovation, appreciative of this effort and remembering how Hannah had hit in other games.

The Purple Panthers pleaded for a base hit. Madelyn was on deck behind Hannah and after Madelyn, the top of the batting order would be up to bat again. If Hannah could only get on base, they had a chance.

Emilee watched the injured girl dig in at the plate. She hoped that Hannah would not be aiming for the fences now, trying to tie this ball game up with a home run for her own personal gain.

Hannah stayed very cool and very calm. She watched a strike go by and then she swung at the next pitch, meeting it solidly. Obviously, Hannah was not trying for a home run because she now understood the importance of just getting on base for her team. The Purple Panthers needed just one base runner.

The ball arched over third and rolled to the left field fence. The crowd screamed again as Hannah hobbled down to first base. This hit would have been a stand up double for anybody else, but Hannah just could not make it that far.

Coach Wilson immediately sent Destiny Johnson in to run for Hannah and Hannah came back to the dugout, limping worse than ever, her face white. However, she had given them the new life that they needed.

Everybody pounded Hannah's back as she came into the dugout. Coach Wilson said quietly,

"Good girl, Hannah. I knew you could do it."

"We can't let you down, coach," Hannah said and Emilee realized something at that moment. This team of girls was killing itself to win this world championship. Maybe they thought they were doing it for their town, for their parents, for themselves, but the real reason was apparent now. They were fighting here, tooth and nail for Coach Wilson, the semi-pro player, who had never been too much as a softball player herself, for this gaunt, kind, homely woman, who loved her team of girls and understood them. It was obvious this team loved and respected their coach too.

The Qiaohui pitcher was very nervous and she walked Madelyn Taylor, putting runners on first and second with one away, Sarah Anderson coming up.

Again, the excitement gripped the Purple Panther players the way it had gripped them every inning before. They had the tying and winning runs on base with the top of the lineup coming up.

Sarah stood at home plate watching the pitcher. Emilee was in the on deck circle, ready to bat next, gripping her bat, crouching, sweating. If Sarah went down it would be up to her to get the Purple Panthers out of this jam.

Sarah did not go down, however. The shortstop hit a single out to left field, and Destiny Johnson, running like the wind, came in to score the tying run. With no cut-off made on the throw to the plate, Madelyn sprinted to third.

It was Moore on first and Taylor on third, with one away, Emilee Davis batting. The Lake Forbing crowd could not make more noise. The game tied up again at 11 to 11, a crazy score in an unbelievable game. Tweets were going crazy on twitter.

Emilee stood at the plate, her nerves calming down. It was impossible they lose now. Nothing could take this victory from them. A team like the Purple Panthers could not lose. They refused to. If the Qiaohui had scored another nine runs in the previous inning, she still would have thought that. The Purple Panthers would not quit and they would never give up. Madelyn screamed to Emilee,

"Bring me home, big sister. Bring me home!"

The Qiaohui pitcher finally pitched to Emilee. She swung at the first pitch and smashed the softball hard, way out to center field. The Qiaohui center fielder went back for it and caught it, but she was in no position to throw Madelyn, who had tagged up at third, out at home. Madelyn Taylor had scored easily from third base with the winning run and the game was over. The Purple Panthers had won and the place went wild!

Emilee came back from first. The entire Purple Panther team was a heaping congregation around home plate. They were pounding Madelyn Taylor's back. Isabella was climbing up on top of the heap. Even the injured Hannah was trying her best to get in on the celebration. Coach Wilson was behind them, watching, grinning.

In the seats behind the Purple Panther dugout, another demonstration was going on. Purple Panther fathers were yelling, shaking hands with each other. J. C. Taylor was pumping Luke Lopez's hand. The mothers were hugging and crying with joy. Reporters with microphones and television cameras appeared from all directions. Everyone wanted in on this moment.

Coach Wilson looked over the heads of the Purple Panther players, at Emilee coming down to join the celebration. Emilee launched into the maelstrom of yelling, joy-crazed players. They pounded her back; they tore off her cap and threw it into the air.

Emilee saw Jasmine Brown on the edge of the heap, waving, laughing, and grinning with her big smile, happy as any girl could be. She saw little girls running out on the field, screaming for Purple Panther autographs.

"Emilee," Jasmine yelled. "We did it, Emilee!"

Emilee waved back at her with tears flowing down her face. She looked across at Coach Wilson, over near the dugout, standing alone. Coach was watching her, smiling.

Coach saw them all together now, Madison Moore and Sarah Anderson, Hannah Miller and Sofia Hernandez, Madelyn Taylor and Isabella Lopez, all of them, every walk of life fused together here in this mass of crazed joy around home plate. They were champions, to themselves, to us all, but most importantly, they were champions to each other.

One thought was running through Coach Jennifer Wilson's mind and Emilee saw it in the coach's eyes. This was good, it was very good, and it was just the beginning of more to come.

## THE END

# APPENDIX: TAKING CARE of YOUR GLOVE OR MITT

How do you make a softball glove or mitt more comfortable, thus more reliable? How do you make one last so you can save yourself lots of time and money? You and I both know that catching or fielding a softball is hard enough. However, it is almost impossible with a stiff glove. We could ask Samantha Smith. Might the ball have popped out of her glove because she had not cared for it properly? Below are a few tips on how to take care of your glove or mitt. Please note that with proper care, your glove or mitt can last for a very long time. With proper care, your glove or mitt could become your best friend, because the longer it stays with you, the more reliable it becomes for those clutch situations. Just like you, your glove or mitt needs training and must stay in excellent physical condition to meet the physical demands of competitive softball. So please, be responsible and read the following. You just never know, playing softball could be your life calling.

1. Start with a can of mink oil. Other oils, lanolin, petroleum jelly, even WD 40 work. However, the tried and true oil for your softball glove is mink oil. Put a few drops of mink oil on a sponge or clean rag. Do not soak the rag or sponge. Too much oil is not good when trying to break-in or condition your softball glove or mitt. PLEASE REMEMBER leather is a "skin." Too much oil, too much sun, or too much moisture is not good for it. Moderation is the key.

2. Work your oiled sponge or rag inside and outside the glove or mitt entirely. Do not forget to work the laces. If you see any excessive amount of oil on the leather, remove it with a dry cloth or towel.

3. Now, take the glove or mitt and twist it, bend it, pound it with your fist in a real effort to make it flexible. Spend at least 10 minutes with this. C'mon, break a sweat!

4. Now, put a softball in the pocket of your glove. Close the glove or mitt around the ball and tie it up with old belts or shoelaces. Keep the mitt wrapped overnight at room temperature. You can even sleep with it if you like. It is okay to show it some respect. Just remember that you CAN NOT leave your glove in extremely hot temperatures, because, just like a skin, it will dry out, even split in extreme cases.

5. Take a wooden mallet or use a small souvenir softball bat for this next step. Unwrap the glove or mitt and remove the softball. Place it on the hand that you do not throw with or your catching hand. Pound the inside of your mitt for about 10 minutes with the mallet or small bat. Use enough force or pressure to replicate a ball hitting your glove.

6. Place the softball back in your glove and tie it up again. Make sure you wrap the glove tight enough so

your softball does not fall out. Let the glove or mitt sit alone or sleep with you overnight at room temperature. This is a good time to show some respect. After all, you just gave it a beating and it still wants to work for you.

7. The next morning, untie your glove and remove the softball. Put the glove on your hand and throw the softball into the glove for at least 10 minutes. Try to throw the ball and catch it in the pocket of the mitt.

8. Find a friend and play catch. Try to catch the softball at least 100 times while you are tossing it back and forth. I have gone to batting cages to practice catching because I do not like chasing errant throws from some of my friends. The pitching machine can throw balls to you and you can adjust the speed while in the cage. However you do it, break a sweat!

9. Keep a softball in your mitt anytime it is not in use. Prevent the palm of the glove or mitt from developing a wrinkle by wrapping it. Play catch frequently to increase your glove's ease of movement and flexibility. Keep your mink oil handy, just do not over do it.

As your glove or mitt ages, with proper care, just like you, it becomes better looking and more reliable. **IT WILL NOT EVER LET YOU DOWN!**

Joe Jackson
**DAMIME PUBLISHING COMPANY**
**P. O. BOX 8453**
**SHREVEPORT, LA. 71108**

Made in the USA
Lexington, KY
23 March 2014